LOVE WORKS LIKE THIS

Lauren Slater

LOVE WORKS LIKE THIS

Moving from One Kind of Life to Another

RANDOM HOUSE

NEW YORK

Library of Congress Cataloging-in-Publication Data

Slater, Lauren.
Love works like this: moving from one kind of life
to another / Lauren Slater.
p.   cm.
ISBN 0-375-50376-5 (alk. paper)
1. Slater, Lauren. 2. Mothers—Biography. 3. Love, Maternal. 4. Pregnancy.
5. Depressed persons—Biography. 6. Depression in women. I. Title.
HQ759.S575 2002
306.874'3'092—dc21   2001058911

Printed in the United States of America on acid-free paper
Random House website address: www.atrandom.com

24689753

FIRST EDITION
Book design by Carole Lowenstein

For my sisters, who understood
And for my daughter, who I hope someday will

ACKNOWLEDGMENTS

Thanks to Ana Cecilia Gonzales, whose expert skill with children has enabled me to do my work; without her help, I would not be able to write. Thanks also to my husband, who has so much love to offer, and to my father, for his humor. My friends, especially Elizabeth Graver, Karen Propp, Pagan Kennedy, Jennifer Coon, and Tracy Slater, read this manuscript in several stages and provided excellent feedback. As always, my editor Kate Medina has allowed me the latitude to explore what interests me, and for that I am grateful. My agent, Kim Witherspoon, has been a huge support. Nell Casey gave me a much needed nudge along the way, and Dr. Alexander Vuckovic, of McLean Hospital, kept me afloat with his knowledge and his care during what was a complex pregnancy; his help was invaluable. Natalie Angier's book *Woman: An Intimate Biography* was an inspiration and resource, as was Abigail Thomas's excellent memoir, *Safekeeping.* I also wish to thank my mother, who reentered my life after a very long hiatus literally as I labored to bring my own child into the world. Her ability to tolerate my written explorations of our relationship is exemplary. She has modeled for me flexibility and forgiveness; I will try to emulate these qualities as I navigate the motherhood that is now mine.

The following is an account of pregnancy. Although broken up by dates, it is not a diary and should not be read as such. It is, rather, something like a travelogue, an attempt to chart one woman's progression through the complex and sometimes compromised months leading up to, and through, early motherhood. I hope it will be of help to, or at least keep company with, women who find themselves in the long wait between conception and parenthood.

LOVE WORKS LIKE THIS

PROGESTERONE

You can hold it in your hand. You can define it, a multipronged sex steroid with an exacting beauty and a mission inscripted in its code. If you peered closely, and if you had, on top of that, excellent eyesight, you could see progesterone, its molecular pattern like a series of tiny tiles forming a ring. The tiles are weightless, and yet indescribably weighty. They are not glass, or clay; they are not granite, and certainly not cement, but they are indescribably weighty, planetary almost, as heavy as the moon, as certain sucks of air that bring down planes and birth big winds, progesterone. Respect it, as a hormone, as a physical force, for it is, she is, the primary chemical of pregnancy—pro-gestation—she is heat.

The first symptom of pregnancy, days before the store-bought test turns its colors, is heat. Under the influence of progesterone your body's temperature edges up as much as one degree. In a body built for homeostasis, that degree is significant. Raise the earth's temperature a simple single degree and the tarmac will melt, the seas swell. Similarly, raise the body's temperature just this tiny increment and it will mean one of two important possibilities. You are fighting an infection. You are building a baby.

Which has, just this minute, slipped down the piping of the fal-

lopian tubes and is burrowing into the uterus. At this point, the baby is very small, smaller than the hormone which sustains it. The baby is a few, marvelous cells, and very unstable. A simple glitch and it will bleed out your openings. Progesterone, on the other hand, is solid. Its cells, like tiny tiles, strong as a suck of wind, it brings the baby down.

The strange thing is, progesterone is so similar to testosterone in its excellent design and yet so different in its spirit. Progesterone is undeniably female. It is, or she is, made not of protein, like the peptide hormones are, but of fat. Many molecular structures in our body are held together by protein, but the sex steroid progesterone is held together at its core by cholesterol, so maybe, in your hand, it has a Crisco quality, maybe it casts not a shadow but a shine.

Like the neurotransmitters—serotonin, dopamine, norepinephrine, which send chemical signals to the brain with a da da dum—progesterone tells your brain—da dum, da dum—to build up the endometrium in the uterus. In this sense, progesterone is not a minimalist hormone. It leans toward excess, toward velvet, toward a thickening of the blood. Under its spell, the womb's endometrial mat goes from a thin brown covering to a thick crimson pile, a wild, expensive carpet, bedding fit for a king. No amount of money could buy a mattress with the thickness, the precision, the pure comfort that progesterone produces, here is where you started your first perfect sleep. Shhh. Every night, when we lie down, we remember this, our original bed. Shhh. Quiet now. Your period is late. Maybe, inside of you, you can hear her coming.

THE FIRST TRIMESTER

September 21, 1998

It is dawn, and I am peeing in a cup. The urine is thick, hot, full of sediment and gold. I dip the test wand in. It reacts immediately, as though it's been burned. The plastic window turns a scalding red and, seconds later, a plus sign swims to the surface. This is a sign unmistakable in its message. Yes yes yes. And yet I don't know how to read the test. I see the cross, a plus. I see the scalding, and think of things that hurt.

I go back into the bedroom, where he sleeps. "It's positive," I say to him. He is Jacob. We are married, but wear no rings. We do not nod to convention. He has always wanted a child. I, on the other hand, have never quite known. I get back between the blankets. He holds me close in his arms. I can feel him smile against my cheek.

I have brought the pregnancy test into the bedroom with me. It sits now on the night table, and while he dozes, I watch it. I want to think about the baby growing inside me, but instead I just listen to the crows outside our window. I wonder where I have put my nail clippers. I wonder why pregnancy tests have the names they do. First Alert. Early Response. Like smoke detectors, is there a fire here? And why do they display their findings in such unimaginative symbols—crosses, dots, slashes? If I could design the perfect pregnancy test, its results would read at once primitive and poetic, an image of a rocking horse for yes, a martini for no. Or this. I have it. The window turns a scalding red. Far away, fires burn in California and whole homes come down. But here, in the East, I am building my home, and the perfect test would flare and words would swim up. If it's negative the test reads, *Keep your excellent life.* If it's positive the test reads, *Risk everything.*

September 26

Pros

Learning a new kind of love

Cons

Less time for friends
less time for work
less money
famous women writers who had children?
Prozac (I'm on it)
mental illness (I have it)
giving birth
sleepless
dreamless

labor, the dusky shar-pei-like folds of the vagina pulled back to reveal the huge hair ball and then the sleeplessness, how the days become a blur and you lose language, your voice growing high and teeny, and you find yourself lost in the world of the cute, and what is cute, really, but the flip side of grotesque?

Barney

Chuck E. Cheese and the huge hulking figures and the grease and

the highways and the waste. Baby gear is waste. It does not decompose. I do not want a stroller. I would rather push my offspring in a wheelbarrow, save me from a stroller, from cute, from bouncies and onesies, from any kind of ending with an *ie*—nappies, binkies, winkies— those little slithering dips at the ends of words signaling a sort of gracelessness, a woman whose neocortex has been temporarily unplugged. In motherhood, I fear words disappear, is there any poetry here? Do brains live here? I want to be a brain, not a body. I never liked my body, but my brain I have some modest hopes for. And I'm drug dependent. Let's not forget that little point, those little pills. My breasts hurt.

Right now, I take off my shirt.

I unsnap my bra.

I am six days into it, according to the test, four and a half weeks according to the timetable used by physicians— LMP—Last Menstrual Period.

My breasts are ready, even if I'm not. They ache deeply and unambivalently. I have lived a life of words, of doctoral degrees, not to mention my feminist leanings, which translate into *Be as much like a man as you can*. So how does a woman who wants to be a man have a baby? And yet there, in the pros column, *"Learning a new kind of love."*

My breasts ache. The nipples, which tend toward inwardness, have lately sprung their moorings. They point ahead, and are extremely tender to the touch.

I touch them. I have always wanted to know what kind of caring I am capable of. Could I care for a child? Could I put someone else's skin before my own?

Risk everything.

And so I touch my nipples. I squeeze them hard, hard, so tears come to my eyes and the ache turns fierce and dark. And here's what happens. Here's the surprise. I'm only six days into it, and I dwell in the column of the cons, and yet today liquid comes out this membranous spigot, a few drops of thick gold—colostrum?—too early for that. So what is it? I don't know. I smear the liquid on my fingers. I lift my fingers to my mouth. And here, in the column of the cons, I discover the taste is surprisingly sweet.

September 28

Study 1

One thousand Prozac-using women continued on the drug throughout the second and third trimesters of their pregnancies. There were no ill effects observed in the babies immediately post birth. Eli Lilly has therefore concluded that, while women should carefully weigh the risks and benefits of drug use in pregnancy, Prozac does appear to be relatively safe.

Study 2

Chambers followed the progress of a group of Prozac-using women from the first trimesters of their pregnancies through the birth of their babies. The study found a statistically significant increase in minor birth defects in Prozac-exposed children. These minor defects suggest possible neurological damage that has yet to be discovered. In addition, the researchers found more immediate postbirth problems in Prozac-exposed babies—extreme jitteriness, respiratory difficulties, and occasional seizures.

Study 3

Women taking Prozac in the first trimester of their pregnancies have a higher risk of spontaneous abortion.

Study 4

A team of researchers followed seventeen Prozac-exposed children in utero through the first seven years of their development and found no difference in social skills or IQ as compared with their peers. The researchers conclude that, in these children at least, Prozac-exposed babies have no neurological sequelae of any significance.

Study (really a story) appearing on the Internet, July 1998, from a woman named Fran

Hello. I am a woman who took sixty milligrams of Prozac a day throughout my pregnancy. Everyone assured me it was safe. You should all be careful, because my baby was born with webbed fingers and toes, which was easy enough to deal with surgically, but still, a web is a web.

I close down my computer, put away my files, and go to bed. It's only noon, in the middle of a bright blue day, but I'm going to bed. I dream of a baby in a sailboat. Then I dream I walk into my kitchen and a thicket of bog grass is growing out of my disposal. I am horrified, but when I go to pull it out I feel how it is hair, and I tug an infant from the plumbing in my sink, and I braid its verdant beauty.

September 30

I am a woman of routine. Every night, before bed, I read at least twenty pages. I always eat a bagel a day. I walk my dogs in two twenty-minute intervals. I carry a PalmPilot, but my sock drawer is a mess.

I sleep in a bra, because it cuts down on dressing time in the A.M., which has to be carried out in very specific seconds. There is a hidden pattern of stars in my ceiling. I trace the six points to appease my gods, who make many demands on me. In the morning, I drink one cup of coffee with two tablespoons of milk. I turn on NPR in the kitchen, the volume dial set to six. Seven is too high, and the news sounds ominous. Five is too low, and the whole world is weightless.

After my bagel and my coffee, I take my pills. I take

four, for the compulsions, and also for the depressions. I line the four up and observe them, every morning. I slug them down with coffee, which enhances their bitterness. Medication is not something to take lightly, I have always believed this to be so. You should collapse the capsule in your mouth. You should tongue its acrid powder. I do this every morning.

Except this morning. I have, you see, pulled a baby from the sink, and braided its beautiful hair. I do everything the same except the pills. All those contradictory studies, and the hair. When it comes time to take the pills, I drop them, one by one, into a large glass of water. Each capsule, made of digestible plastic, slowly bloats, bursts, and powder glitters in the water. I pour the water down the sink, where once the baby was, and then I rise, pregnant and clean.

October 2

By day 30, almost all twenty-three milk teeth are embedded in the gums. Why do I not have nausea?

October 6

"You could write about our mother," my sister says to me.

"Why is that?" I say.

"Because she's the reason," my sister says. My sister, as she speaks, paints her nails. They are long, curved, and she does them in a glittery black.

"She's the reason you're ambivalent about having a child."

"No she's not," I say. "The reason is because of my résumé."

My sister eyes me. She puts her hand under the heat lamp. "Your résumé," she repeats.

"I have an impressive résumé," I say. "I have three advanced degrees and over one hundred publications. I have a demanding job. I work fifty, sixty hours a week. On top of that I try to write my books. Given the choice between writing a book and having a baby, I think I'd rather have the book. Also, of course, there's the mental illness problem."

"And why do you think you have this mental illness problem?" my sister asks. "Any chance it has to do with you know who?"

"Listen," I say. "I've stopped believing in history. I believe in hormones, peptides, and proteins. I believe in molecules, not mothers, okay?"

My sister sighs. Her nails are dry. They have on them a solid inch black lacquer sheath, but somehow, on her, this looks good. "Say that again," she says.

"Say what?"

"That you don't believe in, you know."

"I don't believe in mothers," I say.

"But you're a mother," my sister says.

She's right. I'm a mother, and I don't believe, or even understand, what I suddenly am.

October 7

My first hospitalization occurred when I was fourteen, my last when I was twenty-four. I have devoted exactly one decade of my life to patienthood. On the one hand, that seems like a lot, given that I have been alive only three decades. On the other hand, that one decade is only one-third of my life, and the other two decades are two-thirds of my life, and two-thirds is twice as much as one-third, so I am proportionately healthier, at least time-wise, than I am sicker. Well. Let's just hope, because being a mother and being a mental patient are really mutually exclusive, at least according to the law, and according to private opinion as well. Enough of this. Sometimes, when I sleep, just before I sleep, I see the hospital where I spent one-third of my life. It was not a bad place. It had yellow walls and in the summer was as cool as a vintage wine cellar. Once, my father came to visit me there, on a hot July day, and we sat outside and the air smelled thick from fruit trees, grass so green it cut my eyes to see it, and my father put his hand on my head, and he said, "Lauren, all I ever want for you is peace of mind."

October 9

Still no nausea. Are my hormones high enough?

October 17

No nausea. No symptoms. Oh God. Thank God.

October 20

Jacob and I go out for breakfast. I feel fantastic. The day is fantastic, a snap in the air, mums and pumpkins piled high in people's gardens. Today I order three blueberry pancakes with warmed syrup, and I taste each blueberry as though it's brand-new, bursting like ink in my mouth.

It is the kind of day when you really must be outside. I take the dogs to the woods, where we will hike. "Be careful," Jacob says to me, for the woods near where we live are a cruising ground for gay males. Five years ago a man was murdered, found in the stream. Ten years ago a pair of lovers never returned.

I enter the thicket of trees. I smell water. The summer has been a wet one, and all the bogs are brimming. The streams are gurgling, giving off a silvery vapor. My nose feels absolutely alive, like it's separate from my face, its own little humming unit, it takes in odors and breaks them down into their component parts: the silvery water, which is fish skin, mercury, silt, and damp stone; the red-gold leaf I press to my nostrils, pepper and bark; the earth, which is everything, rottenness, ruin, all rising up to meet me.

I walk the path. Up ahead, the trees thicken and close, blocking out the sun. I lift my face to the sky and scent the sun; it is surprisingly strong, like gas and lemons, I go down.

A gale of nausea sweeps over me, and I am utterly surprised by its swiftness, my stomach seizing up, I retch and retch; *okay*, I think, *enough*, I think, and then, just like that, it's over.

I straighten, a little shaky, wipe my mouth with the back of my hand. "Musashi!" I call, "Lila." My voice wavers, all broken and fantastically fragile—I am pregnant!—and before me stands a man, smiling.

"You all right?" he asks. He is wearing the tiniest pair of shorts I have ever seen, and no shirt at all. He has the requisite earring in one ear, a little gold dollop, and his hair is straight seventies, feathered and soft.

"I'm fine," I say, smiling at him. "I'm, I'm pregnant," I say proudly, gesturing vaguely toward the mess I've made on the ground.

"Pregnant," he says, and then he nods. "Yup."

I can't wait to go home and tell Jacob. The excitement is just now beginning to build. I have arrived. I am just so pleased, so tickled, so pink, so silly. This man, my witness, is suddenly so special to me. It does not matter that he wears no shirt in October, that his shorts ride up in his crotch, contouring a bulge too big to be believed. It does not matter than he has a scar on his stomach, oddly cesarean, a pink welt at the bikini line. The excitement is suddenly racing through me, making me tremble, and my nose feels very alive.

"I'm eight weeks pregnant," I say. "It's a hassle."

"Oh I know, I know," he says. "I'm pregnant too."

"You too?" I say, beginning to laugh. I could laugh and laugh—something is wrong here, but it's too much fun—the ease of my laughter, lubricated and high, I am slippery, slipping, two weeks now without my medication.

"It's not funny," he says, touching his scar.

"Oh I know," I say, and I switch into seriousness, we are dead serious here, there is nothing funny. Someone, somewhere, suffers.

"You don't believe me," the man says, and looks sad.

"No," I say, "of course not. Only women get pregnant."

He shakes his head. He looks genuinely mournful, harmless. I want to help him. Crazy people rarely scare me, they are my bread and butter after all, and in their skin I sense myself. Myself, slipping, thrilled, I want to help the whole world.

"Touch my stomach," he says, "and you'll see."

"Okay," I say, and I do, I touch his stomach, hard as slate, and he moves my hand down, down, and I start to get scared now, sensible now, I thought he was gay, so why is he moving my hand down, down, and then he stops at his scar, just above the belt line.

And sure enough I feel it, deep in this man's belly, a tiny

flutter, very fast, or is that just his pulse, my pulse? I jerk away, back away. "Musashi!" I call. "Lila!" I call. I am sound again, sane again; the dogs come bounding back and we are running, running out of the woods and into the light, which feels too bright, solid chunks of light, a clashing sound, coyotes. Howl.

October 31

My moods are all over the place. The books say to expect that in the first trimester, when your hormones are wild, but this is much more than I bargained for. I drive to work in tears. I press a washcloth over my nose to keep out the sickening scents. The world is grainy, like an old film clip.

Today, walking the dogs, I passed a playground. It looked bad, a place of pillories with holes to put the heads. Children raced around, screaming, and mothers sat, each one staring into the air.

I went home, and sought my study. Where in my careful world is there room for a child to grow? What losses will I incur? I cry and cry. Outside the sun migrates across the sky, puddles down.

And then he is there. "Are you okay?" he says. "Tell me," I say, "about the solar system," because I want to know a world beyond the female flesh, a world of hard facts and hugeness, something one can compute.

He comes in. He is always happy to respond to any sort

of scientific request. He once said that if he could carry a whiteboard with him everywhere, he would feel fulfilled in life. "The solar system," he says, standing by the day-bed, assuming a lecturing pose.

I watch him. He has a red-blond beard. His eyes glitter behind tiny glasses. He appears to be a man with no fear. I have poked him here and I have poked him there and I have been unable to find his fear. With my husband, I have never been so soothed and so separate at the same time.

November 13

Because I am a psychologist, I know all the signs. Disturbed sleep. Disturbed appetite. Neurovegetative symptoms. Psychomotor retardation. It is difficult to move; my limbs say no. I stand at the stop of the stairs, holding on with one hand to the newel post, looking down the slant, and considering. I spend a long time weighing the pros and cons of staying put, or descending. The decision feels tricky and enormous.

All the signs above are symptoms of depression. They are also, however, symptoms of pregnancy, so maybe I'm not depressed. Maybe I'm just pregnant. Maybe to be pregnant is to be depressed. Then would the converse also be true, that to be depressed is to be pregnant? Of course not! Why can an equation work one way but not the other? Why does two plus two always equal four, but four is not necessarily the same as two plus two? Why, if Tamiflu cures the flu, is the flu not caused by lack of Tamiflu? My brain swims in my head; the questions are intense.

I make a decision. I get to the bottom of the stairs. Musashi comes over and licks my knee. He keeps licking and licking my knee in one specific spot and at last I see why. I have skinned my knee, with blood and all. I don't know how this happened. Perhaps I fell down the stairs, although I highly doubt it. In any case, the hows do not matter, only the whys. Why Musashi licks my knee is because there's blood on it, I have an answer. I have an answer! His tongue looks pretty, a flickering red, but I know it's full of germs. I should push him away from the cut, but I don't. I cannot find it in myself to care.

What I find in myself is a fatigue that flees during the night so I am wide awake and blinking, and descends during the day, without warning, each nap a small, delectable death.

"It's back," I say to Jacob, the it being illness, and being housed in hospitals; the hospitals are coming back. I thought they were behind me but I was wrong. Inside me now there is a coiled thing going from parasite to personhood and as it does it emits its toxins. I hear voices. I have a hyperawareness. There, on the floor, lies a needle, shining like the highest wheedling note of a violin. People's faces look funny, in so many separate pieces, the isolated mouth moving, the simple blink of an eye excruciating, the silky crash of lashes. What a weird, hallucinatory world.

The sun is an assault. I am, by the way, on the street,

taking a walk or running an errand. I have a new under-standing. When it comes to mental illness there is no such thing as history. There is never a recovery; there are only remissions, come and go. Seesaw. The crows caw. Perhaps I should get an abortion.

Can a mentally ill woman be a good mother? It's such a sane question; I'd like to take a poll. A woman walks by me pushing her carriage, one of those ridiculous double-wheeled canopied gizmos, equipped with mesh storage pockets in every possible place. "Are you mentally ill?" I say, and she says, "Yes, but only at certain times," and I say, "What times?" and she says, "Noontimes, and then I am fine," and just like that, she fizzles away. Noontimes, she says. Sometimes, I say. Sometimes I have it, and I take medication for it, and, yes, I have been hospitalized for years of my life, and then other times, remission, I'm fine. Should a woman like that become a mother? How will she mother at noontime?

I go home. Jacob returns. Key in the lock. Door opens. "What is it?" he says.

"I'm not fit to be a mother," I say. "Once a mental patient always a mental patient. Look at me."

So he does. Jacob has never seen me go down, because for our entire relationship I've been maintained on medi-cation.

"You shouldn't have gone off the drugs," he finally says.

"Well, I did," I say.

"You're not as bad as you think," Jacob says.

"Listen," I say. "I got pregnant because I thought the illness was under control. But it never will be. I can't mother with this handicap."

"So don't," he says.

"Abortion?" I say.

"No," he says. "So don't mother. Who says just because you have the child you have to mother it. I'll raise the child myself."

His response takes the wind right out of my agitated sails. "You will?" I say.

"I will," he says, but he looks sad.

"What role will I play?" I ask.

"Incubator," he says.

"But after that?" I say.

He shrugs. "I want a child. If you can't take it on, I'll do it myself. I'll hire help."

"But I'll have to be something," I say. "How about if I'm the father and you're the mother? We'll switch."

Jacob stands still, considering this. "No," he says. "I've always wanted to be a father. I've never wanted to be a mother."

"Well, maybe I've always wanted to be a father too," I say.

Jacob smiles. I smile, for I see how silly this is, and yet at the same time how utterly sober, how sociologically complex, a Goffman drama.

"You can be the aunt," Jacob says.

"Aunt," I say, trying out the word. I've always liked that word. It reminds me of ant, ants, my favorite insects.

"I could be the aunt," I say, excitement mounting, for I

can see my way out of this dilemma, and it's on the segmented black back of an ant.

"Well then, will we have sex anymore?" I say. "The father's not supposed to sleep with the aunt."

"We'll have sex," he says.

"So we're not breaking up," I say.

"No," he says, "we're not breaking up."

I spend the rest of the evening awash in relief, which feels like its own kind of chemical pumping through me, at first soothing and then staccato. My pace picks up, I have found a way out. I am very excited. I wash all the floors, sponge down the baseboards, consider the architecture of our home. It's a single family, but with a little bit of work, a wall or two, some soundproofing, we could turn the third floor into a separate apartment where the aunt would live amidst books and metaphors, occasionally descending to dine with Dad, to rock the baby, everything hazy and scented, katydids thronging in the grass.

I fall asleep with blueprints on my mind, but by the time I wake up, at four in the morning, I know the fantasy's over. I just forgot about my body for a little while, but now my body's back, and it sends its undeniable signals, breasts aching at their roots, uterus aflutter. You can never be *just incubator.* I've spent years learning to think linearly, statistically, logically, learning to separate and segment, but motherhood will not cooperate. It will not be just biological. The child is yours not because you bore it in your womb but because every physical symptom gave rise to an image—it is moving now, the heart beats now—the child is yours because you have imagined it, a girl, maybe, with dark eyes and a bright bow of a mouth, or a boy with shoe polish black hair, it does not matter. There is no force which can claim you like imagination can, a force, I find, which brings nothing into something and insists that you acknowledge your authorship. Our children are not ours because we have given them our genes. They are ours because we have had the audacity to envision them.

November 14

No, I don't want to say what she did. No, her hands were not, no, the red rip of her mouth, I don't want to say that. Mother. The tiny car. I don't remember this. I don't remember that. Yes, I do remember Florida, wasn't that pretty, the ocean of the palest green, the oily black sea urchin in a puff of sharpness? Do you remember those things? I do. Sometimes she surprised us. There were these quick, wind-whipped gestures of kindness, I want to remember those. A woman of substantial rage, yes. But then there was Florida, and the bridal white beach she walked on barefoot, with so much hope. What I want to hang on to in my mother are the moments when her second self appeared. Once, in Florida, we were on the beach. Suddenly, the lifeguard blew his whistle hard. "Jellyfish, jellyfish!" he screamed. "Everyone clear out!" and there they were, the jellyfish, moving through the Floridian sea like a large dark stain, and the whole beach backed away except our mother, who went toward the metastasizing mass in the water, her hands stretched out. What did she want with that? She was not afraid of darkness, being dark herself. Or she craved the sleek energy of free fish, she, a straight-backed housewife. She went forward. The world went back. She went in. The world went out. The jellyfish swam around her, craziness, courage, a little bit of both.

This memory is for my sister, the keeper of complexities.

November 18

There are trees everywhere. When we moved into this house, five years ago, it was appropriately landscaped, but we have let it go. The holly trees are vicious, bearing their berries like blisters. The oaks oppress me, so muscular and judgmental. I call a tree man. "I want you to take every last branch away," I say.

"These trees are part of the place," he says. "Are you crazy?"

"Yes," I say, and that shuts him up, very fast.

We stand together then, surveying the yard. "Nice yard," he says at last.

"Every last branch," I say, "okay?"

"You could sue me later," he says, "when you're no longer crazy."

"When will that be?" I say and the tree man looks at me. At night, now, I am hearing a voice or two. I rarely get out of bed; I have taken a leave from work. There are many moths in my house, in my head, I'm not sure which.

"When will that be?" I ask again.

The tree man shrugs. He doesn't know. No one knows.

November 20

Her office is in the suburbs, her waiting room filled with articles on PMS, on mental illness in menopause, on postpartum psychosis and the birth control pill. She calls me in.

She is very young, and she wears braces, and I am not happy about their presence. As a general policy I don't take guidance from anyone who wears any kind of orthodontic device; it smacks of adolescence.

She smiles at me, and her tracks gleam. Her hair is dark, pulled back in a taut little bun, granny style, as though that might lend her the look of leadership.

I start to speak. I tell her the whole sorry story of my pregnancy. I tell her all about my ambivalence, my thinking about abortion, my fear that I am more male than female, my single, pointed pursuit of words, my heart's desire, which is to make not babies but books. I go into great detail about the effects of seventies feminism on women in the eighties and nineties, how I have so purposefully structured my life to oppose the traditional motherhood role, and it is this conflict which has triggered, if not outright caused, my collapse. I tell her about my history of collapses, the mental hospitals, et cetera. As I speak she takes notes, which, narcissist that I am, makes me speak all the more quickly, and then she says, "Shhhh.

"You're talking very rapidly," she says. "Do you have any history of bipolar?"

"I have anxiety and depression," I say, "or maybe an agitated depression, which seems to be rooted in my ambivalence—"

She interrupts. "Have you," she says, "ever taken the birth control pill?"

Well now, there's a question I can answer. "Yes," I say.

"And how did you tolerate it?" she asks.

"I couldn't stand it," I say. "I lasted three days. Made me cry nonstop."

She nods, because now she has her answer. She has the answer! Her braces vanish. All I can see now are her shiny teeth, her snappy eyes.

"I don't think you should get an abortion," she says. "Some women are extremely sensitive to progesterone, which in both animal analogues and human studies can cause severe mood reactions."

And then she goes on to tell me that at this stage in my pregnancy I am ingesting the equivalent of *four hundred* birth control pills a day, so it's no wonder I'm losing my mind. "No," she says, "you're not ambivalent, or, rather, your ambivalence is hormonally driven. We see this kind of ambivalence all the time in psychiatrically vulnerable women. The good news is," she says, "once the placenta takes over and the ovaries are out of the picture, at the end of the first trimester, the psychiatric symptoms lessen."

At this point, I'm quite confused by what she's saying—placenta, ovaries, progesterone—although later I will, on my own, read about the bizarre effects sex steroids can have on the emotional pathways in a woman's brain. I will read that it is well documented, among perinatal psychiatrists, that women who have a hard time tolerating the birth control pill, or who experience depression or anxiety premenstrually, or who evidenced a mood disorder at the onset of puberty, are at especially high risk not only during the postpartum period but in the actual pregnancy itself. This is, in fact, so well documented in the perinatal psychiatric literature that I can't believe no one mentioned antenatal depression to me, and to who knows how many other women who decide to carry a child. I read the statistics, that 10 to 15 percent of all pregnant women experience what's called antenatal depression, oftentimes severe, sometimes psychotic, and that these women have an 80 percent chance of developing an incapacitating postpartum reaction as well. So here's the truth, if there is such a thing. Pregnancy can be treacherous for a woman. If there were a food out there that 10 to 15 percent of the population had an adverse response to, someone would put a warning on the label, but there is no warning on the label of pregnancy although, I think, there should be.

"But why?" I say, and then stop, back up. I'm confused.

"At the end of the first trimester?" I say. "You mentioned the depression would go away."

"Yes," she says. "It should, or at least lessen."

"Why?" I say. "Do progesterone levels drop at the end of the first trimester?"

"Oh no," she says, "they continue to rise, right up until you give birth. Oh no. By the end of your pregnancy you'll be ingesting," and here her voice drops a tad, to add a dash of shading to her tone, "you'll be ingesting by the end the equivalent of one thousand birth control pills a day. Imagine that," she says, shaking her head. "Imagine what the liver has to process."

I do. Imagine that. I imagine standing in a bathroom downing fistfuls of Ortho-Novum, pink plastic packets scattered at my feet.

She continues. "Your progesterone levels rise, but the hormone, in the second and third trimesters, is produced by the placenta, not the ovaries. And the placenta makes a gentler form of progesterone. In addition, estrogen kicks in, and that's a mood enhancer."

I nod. I see. I don't. Progesterone, apparently, comes in different flavors, like chocolate and vanilla, like milk, regular, fat free. This is how I explain it to myself, the only way I can. In the first trimester the ovaries produce a thick, clotted kind of progesterone, a white gunk that clogs up the ravines in the brain, but the progesterone from the placenta is light like skim milk, cleansing and translucent.

"Unfortunately," the doctor now says, "the depression

does go away, but it can come back, at the very end of the third trimester, and your risk for a postpartum crisis is extremely high."

"And yet you're telling me," I say, "not to get an abortion."

"This is a time," she says, "of rapid advancement in the treatment of these illnesses. We have many medications, and more and more are getting developed each day. It is," she says, "an auspicious time to bring a child into the world."

I squint at her. Could it really be that all this turmoil is mostly hormonally driven? Is there not any significant way in which my reaction to motherhood is sociological, is psychological?

Her prescription for me is to go back on the Prozac at a megadose, 120 milligrams, plus add lithium and Klonopin into the mix. She tells me about possible risks to the fetus, but I cannot concentrate. "If you choose not to aggressively medicate," she says, "I predict, given your prior history and your current status, that you will be back in a hospital within a few weeks. If you do choose to aggressively medicate, you have a fifty percent chance of feeling better very soon," she says.

"Lithium?" I say.

And then I say nothing at all.

"Lithium?" Jacob says. "You have to go on lithium?" Because he is a chemist by trade, we have an old *Physicians'*

Desk Reference on hand, and so we look it up—lithium—"In humans, lithium carbonate may cause fetal harm when administered to a pregnant woman. Data from lithium birth registries suggest an increase in cardiac and other anomalies."

We look at each other grimly. We look up Klonopin. "The effects of Klonopin in human pregnancy are unknown. . . . When Klonopin was administered to pregnant rabbits . . . a non-dose-related incidence of cleft palates, open eyelids, fused sternebrae and limb defects was observed."

We call back the doctor, together, I on one extension, he on the other. Jacob starts with the heart.

"The cardiac abnormalities, called Ebstein's syndrome, are thought to be overplayed," she says. "Of course we can't be sure, but we can be sure that your wife is ill and that she deserves proper treatment. Every woman does," the doctor says.

"And the Klonopin," Jacob says, "the fused sternebrae, the open eyelids . . ."

She pauses for a moment. The pause to me seems significant, a gap in which twisted things swim. "You mean the bunny studies," she says, "right?"

"Right," Jacob says, his voice low.

"One important thing to remember," she says, "pregnant bunnies are not the same as pregnant humans. I myself have overseen several Klonopin pregnancies and the babies were fine, a little sleepy but fine."

We hang up, meet in the middle of the house. "I'm going to do it," I say.

I expect him to say, "No," to say, "It's my child too, don't I have a choice?" or "Let's consider all the risks versus all the benefits," but instead he just looks at me for a long time, and in his look I see the woman I have now become. "I guess you should," he says.

And so I do, that night. And so I do. I fill the prescriptions, the scored lithium pill, the jazzy orange Klonopin, plus six bicolored bullets of Prozac, I take it all.

And we say nothing. The lithium leaves its salty aftertaste, the Klonopin careens down the dark chute of my body. I am surprised by how little Jacob and I say, how we do not debate the obvious—fetal versus maternal rights, at what point personhood begins, culturally embedded ideas about drugs versus their chemical reality—no, not once do we discuss these topics, although I know they are on our minds. Later on, we will, I will, go over and over the path I pursued, while I watch my child sleep, while I pray she opens her fist for the rattle, I will see the Klonopin darting down into the darkness of my bowels, while we hope she crawls with a hope so much like that of other parents, but more, a hope underscored with anxiety and blame, later on.

After she is born.

December 18

And then, of course, there's the other side to the selfish story. I go to the library and read what I can. It is snowing today, fine white crystals falling from the sky, the sky itself as hard as a block of salt except in one tiny place where the pale sun struggles to break through. I love libraries in winter. I love the steam heat hissing, the glow of burnished wood, the silence of the inside world mingling with the silence of the snow beyond the thick-paned windows.

I've been on the lithium for a few weeks now, and I am noticing a difference. An appreciation of the weather. A kind of calmness that may or may not be resignation. It is in this state that I see the other side of the selfish story.

I read. A study by Carol Dix found that 30 to 80 percent of women with preschool children experience depression. A second study found that a woman's mental health appears to decline after she marries and bears children, whereas a man's tends to increase. According to Susan Maushart, females are a whopping sixteen times more likely to experience psychosis after the birth of a child, and pregnancy for a woman with a history of depression is a known and serious psychiatric risk.

I am about thirteen weeks pregnant now. My breasts are, depending on your point of view, either spectacular or perverse, globular and wired with veins; they glow.

I go back outside. It is nearing Christmastime and hundreds of women move through the dusk. I stand on the library steps and watch them, and I feel a new respect. Ninety-four percent of the world's women bear children, which means they agree, knowingly or not, to navigate the most difficult terrain of the brain. Sometimes I am ashamed of being female, but not today. I like the snow, I like the salt-block sky, I like how we women move, en masse, toward the lighted trees.

December 28

The lithium makes me thirsty. The Klonopin helps me sleep. The thirst is tremendous and healing, gallons of cold water going in me, my heart calmed in a cool sea.

Today, just after Christmas, I go into a store called Cherry, Webb & Touraine. Outside it is cold and gray, inside lit and hushed, women wafting the aisles trailing expensive silk scarves, suede skirts. Salesladies stand behind Lancôme counters, the pressed eye powder as appealing as sweets, rose and ice blue.

"A sample of our newest scent?" a woman in an apron asks, and I offer her my naked wrist, the scent very mild, without edge or fire. The perfume smells of laundry, of sprinklers in the evening.

I do not go to my usual spots, the petites, the cosmetics, the accessories. I go, furtively, to the children's section of the store, where infant clothes hang on racks. I look around me to make sure no one is watching, although what the secret is I can't say. I feel enormously self-conscious handling these tiny outfits, these hooded gowns like what a miniature monk might wear. I finger the frills on a little dress. There is a study that scares me. Schizophrenic mothers were compared with depressed mothers and it was found that the schizophrenic women were more effective as parents, because even though they were crazy as bats, at least they were responsive.

And I think of that study, standing very still in a store at Christmastime, holding an infant's dress in my hand and finding it definitely not cute. I dislike cute things, and yet I am no longer crying, no longer thrashing about for breath. *I will design my own kind of motherhood, a different kind of motherhood*, this is what I think. *Please, God, make me well enough to love whoever she is.* This is also what I think. I think the medications must be working, for my thoughts are clear, my mood even, my apprehensions deep but with a bottom.

January 15, 1999

Even-keeled. That's a sailboat in the summer. Recovering. That's a bed in a white room, a glass of fresh squeezed lemonade on the night side table. That's me, walking about in this winter world very, very tentatively, stepping on frozen puddles, considering them when they crack.

I go in for my amnio today. Jacob goes with me. We ride together in the car. The snow is lumpy and dirt-streaked, and ravens rise from the plowed mounds, crying high into the sky.

First, before the needle, we meet with a counselor. We say no to Tay-Sachs, to spina bifida, to cerebral palsy, to

Huntington's, all the ways in which a body, a brain, can twist. I tell her, of course, about my own small-scale twistings, the eight pills I take each day, and as I do my heart paddles fast, and then it's over. I regain my delicate balance.

Jacob and I are taken to a room, I climb up on the table, they do the ultrasound, scanning fast for defects. "Looks good," they say, "so far," and I nod.

"What's the sex?" I say. "Can you see the sex?"

"A girl," the doctor says, "probably a girl," and rain rises up in me then, a kind of drenched grieving happiness, unlike feelings I have ever had.

They are not wonderful feelings, not rosy or glowing. I would not even really recommend them, but there they are. There she is, my mother with her glittery eyes, her wants so huge they drove her down, and me, with my brown eyes, trying for both our sakes to live a largeness she could not, and she, the fetus, with her eyes sealed shut, spinning me on, spinning me out until I no longer exist. We no longer exist, and yet I am not nothing today. I am with child today, powerful.

I feel the punch of the needle in my stomach, see the amniotic fluid rise into the syringe, so much they take, a pearly viscous fluid coming up. "Give me that," I want to say. I want to drink the fluid, swallow all these stem cells, and grow myself, my mother, young again. A second chance.

But instead there is water in a little pleated cup and then home, in my own bed, on the alert for a miscarriage.

I pull out her picture, which they printed for me, here she is. Eyes sealed shut. Spinning us out into nothing, which is everything, every risk and every benefit, every kind of collision and redemption, too much to count. Too many possibilities to hold in a single head. Why I'm going forward in the face of such ambivalence I don't know: blind faith, Jacob, courage, conviction, conformity, stupidity, confusion. Let her escape all this. Of course she won't. I will call her Eva, which in Hebrew means life, and Claire, for clarity, and I will hope the gap between her name and her life is small.

Clear life. A life without illness of the mind. This is what she means, this girl. I study her now. The picture is really good. She lies as though in a hammock, slung comfortably in the pouch of my womb. I can see the profile of her nose, one hand floating palm up as though in resignation, or acceptance. Apparently, this girl is made from me. She comes from me. She has half my genes, half my toxins, half my talents, she is in me. What of me will she shed, what will she find herself tacked to? The gift of life. What an odd expression, a still odder gift, this box of snakes and daisies.

Now I touch her hand. She grips mine. "All right," I say. "Connected," she says, and for better or worse that's certainly true, connected at a level deeper and more dangerous than is wise, and our hands come together. We want to help each other out. I feel the tiny condensed fingernails, the braid of her breathing tube; she touches my mouth and I smile. This is not maternal love I'm feeling.

We want to help each other out. This is not maternal love—no coos or cuteness—it's saner than that, I'm sane for now, and I am not my mother, and my name is Lauren and I look at Eva and I feel the best of what a woman has to offer. I feel friendship.

ESTROGEN

Estrone. Estradiol. Estriol. Sixty different forms of the sex steroid estrogen live inside our bodies. We are awash. The world is awash. Molds make estrogen, soy makes estrogen; I once heard that bobcats, bats, and zebras secrete such high quantities their piss can germinate a garden seed in six hours. Estrogen has so many myths, so many claims to fame, and defame, that where does one begin its tricky tale? First discovered by? Causes cancer in? Sexes the fetal brain with its imperious fingertips? Estrogen. Form over function. It swims on the scientist's specially prepared slide, illuminated by a black light, surprisingly delicate for all its life force, a fragile flake of a molecule, and the molecule most loved by the body. We have receptors for estrogen everywhere inside us, not just on our ovaries but on our bones, our muscles, our brains, our tongues.

Estrogen serves its purposes, all of which are crucial. This hormone strengthens the heart, thickens the blood, clears cholesterol from the arteries, and ignites our cells so all the body gets a buzz. At the time of ovulation, when estrogen briefly peaks, a woman's reflexes quicken. Estrogen turns the tongue nimble, lubricates our language so for a short time each month part poet we are, even if we don't know it.

A normally cycling woman has 146–500 picograms of estrogen in her body that crest and trough at different times during the day and month. A pregnant woman, however, by the second trimester, when estrogen begins her magisterial climb, has many times that, which is why her skin may have that pinkish tinge, and her orgasms pack more of a punch. Estrogen, also, is a known antidepressant, administered in experimental trials to the postmenopausal melancholy in place of Prozac, with some good results. In its liquid form, trapped in a test tube, estrogen, not surprisingly, has a halo kind of color, and drips thick as sap over the lip of the sterilized glass.

Estrogen is hard to figure. It's been, as author Natalie Angier points out, eulogized and demonized. Too much can cause cancer. Too little and you shrivel. The pregnant woman, however, need not concern herself with estrogen's mixed marketing campaign. She needs estrogen absolutely, unambivalently, or at least her fetus does. It is because of estrogen that the fetal cells proliferate into ever more complex structures like heart, like spleen, like the little maroon liver that sifts out toxins; and the toxins you take in, even the undrugged among us, air, water, microscopic particles of lead; the list goes on.

And it is because of estrogen that the pregnant woman's breasts emerge as feeding station, two external placentas. Estrogen stimulates the dormant nodules in the breasts so they sprout an ever-increasing webwork of branches through which the milk can flow. Estrogen softens the breasts' lobular sacs, and then darkens the aureoles so they glow like tavern signs in the night: stop here. On tap.

In pregnancy, estrogen is made, primarily, by the placenta. This may be why the placenta has such lore attached to it, all over the world. Estrogen. Estrus. The crux of life. After birth, some cultures bury the placentas. They bury those estrogen-drenched organs be-

neath dirt huts, in their farming fields, high on mountaintops, deep in ditches, but in the end, you just can't cover estrogen. Scientists once did an experiment. They dug up the placentas of women three months postpartum. Under the influence of estrogen, the placentas had continued to grow, the villi-like projections extending outward for thirty miles underground. Think of that, while you touch your stomach. Pay homage to this hormone. Do your own experiment now, in the relative calm of pregnancy's midpoint. Piss in a cup. This should not be hard, given your gravid state. Then piss in another cup, until you have enough to fill a vase. Tell your honey to bring you home a white rose. Put it in your piss. Go away. Wait two days. Come back. The rose will be stained a vivid inner-lip pink. The room will stink. You may be amazed. You may feel happy. You may also feel a little fear.

THE SECOND TRIMESTER

January 25

Yes, things have changed for me. I cannot go skating and I am scared of walking on ice, but I feel, nevertheless, that I have a better balance. Hormones. Drugs. Word repetition. I have returned to work. I have said the word *mother* to myself so many times it is starting to lose its shock. I lie awake at night and do what people do. I stare at the ceiling. I listen to the rain. I say *mother* one hundred times or more. *Mother mother mother mother.* No matter how many times I utter the word, it will not lose its shape, like, for instance, the word *cucumber,* which collapses by the seventeenth repetition. *Mother* keeps its meaning and its figure. Nevertheless, repeat any word enough and it will cease to alarm you. *Mother mother mother mother.* Slowly, so slowly, I am growing used to its weight on the tip of my tongue, its echo and its shape.

Tonight, lying awake, I decide to do a new variation of the word repetition trick. I get up and pee. The baby has just begun to move in me, little whispery swishes that feel sometimes like hunger. I go to the kitchen. On a piece of browned toast I pen the word *Mother* with a dull knife dipped in rich, soft butter. Then I eat the word. I take it in, in all its grease and brightness.

January 27

Do not believe most of what you read. For instance, morning sickness is an all-day affair. Pregnancy is as dangerous as driving a car, if you have a certain sort of mind. But the books are right about at least one thing, and that is the calmness that comes in the second trimester, ushered in, perhaps, by estrogen, the gravid woman ever so slightly inebriated on this greasy cocktail; I go swimming. I put on my black suit and my stomach shows itself, a small bulge. The YMCA is housed in an old brick building, asbestos flaking off the pipes somewhere in the cellar, it does not matter to me. I walk down the steps of the pool, the tiles slick, the drain a tiny silver point warbling way out, in the deep end, and I float. Inside me the fetus floats. I put my arms out; she puts her arms out. I do the crawl. She does the crawl. For forty minutes each day we are in the same substance, and then I dive for the drain, go as deep as I can, hunched, here, in a place without breath, the world above sealed off by a blue membrane.

I go to the Y for this liquid immersion, but also for the locker room. Every morning before I go off to work it is flooded with women coming from water exercise class. The women are all old, and they are a part of my practice. They snap the rubber caps off their skulls with a sucking sound, and underneath their damp curls lie coiled. When they strip off their suits I see how their flesh has gone fetal thin, how their breasts have been used, how their hips have been widened by baby after baby. I try to read suggestion in their skin. I want to ask them *What was it like, did you ever miss your old, childless self, how did love happen, tell me.*

And then today, an old lady does. She tells me. Her hands are arthritic and she asks if I would lotion up her back, her arms, and then at last her neck, which is spectacularly wattled and loose. I dollop the white cream onto my palm, work it in swaths across her shoulders, over the rough grid of elderly elbows, and then at last to her throat, where the wattles are. I have never touched a wattle before. It feels like pudding and velvet. I have the urge to kiss it. Somewhere, in the back of my mind, memories stutter on—a star, a cat, a lawn of undulating grass.

"Thank you," she says.

My hands shine.

"You know," she says, looking at my belly, "I think you're going to be just fine."

February 3

Jacob and I go to see the psychopharmacologist together. "We consider your wife high-risk," she says, "not only because of the drugs but because of the postpartum period."

"We'll hire help," I say to Jacob in the car, on the way back home.

"Of course we will," he says. "Not only are you crazy. You also have a career."

So, this afternoon, I phone in to an agency. "How old is your child?" a woman who introduces herself as Georgette asks me.

"Well," I say, "she's about twenty weeks," and then I add, "in utero."

"And she already needs a nanny?" Georgette asks.

"I like to get things done ahead of time," I say.

"You new mothers," Georgette says, laughing. "You're all so anxious. Let me tell you," she says, "it's way too early to begin a nanny search. Call us once the baby's born."

"I need," I say, "to have help in place as soon as the baby's born, so I have to start early."

"It's too early," Georgette says.

"Listen," I say. "I, I have an illness. It's extremely important that I am assured I have help."

"Oh," says Georgette. There's a pause on the line. Then she does the unthinkable. "May I ask what's wrong?" she says softly.

I want to say no you may not, my brain is wrong my soul is sunk that cliché called depression, don't let its familiarity fool you, but instead it just flies out of my mouth, I say, "Breast cancer."

"Breast cancer," Georgette repeats.

I don't, you see, know how else to explain.

"Yes," I say.

"I'll fax you our four top candidates right away," she says.

And so she does.

February 11

It snowed today. It was so cold the hairs inside my nose iced over. I went outside and stood under the sky. Each flake was so finely formed, six-pronged, molecular, the whole world releasing fresh sex steroids, mounding up on the ground.

February 13

I am growing weary of my husband. I conceived in September, but this baby has yet to take root in him. I put birth books, pregnancy books, name books on the stand by the bed, and he eschews them for texts on semiotics. At night, as we lie side by side, I glare at him across the sheets. "Listen," I say. "We have to name her. We're calling her Eva, okay?"

"Eva," he says. "I once knew an Eva. She had lupus."

"So then you pick a name," I say.

"Jalopy," he says.

"Don't be stupid," I say.

"Tungsten," he says.

"We are not naming our child Tungsten," I say.

"It's a beautiful name," he says. "It's one of my favorite elements."

"Lily," I say.

"Wolfram," he says.

"It's a girl," I say.

"But you're such a dog lover," he says. "Let's give her some canine characteristics, to help the bonding process."

"Charlotte," I say.

"Isn't that the name of a pig?" he says.

"It's the spider," I say.

"You want to name our daughter after a spider?" he says. "Come on."

"No you come on. Get serious." I snatch the semiotics book out of his hands. "Listen," I say. "We're going to be parents. No more fun and games. We have to grow up."

"I am grown up," he says.

"You have to start cleaning up the house," I say. "You have to stop smoking pot."

"I'm a chemist," he says. "I smoke pot for experimental purposes."

"I'm not leaving my child with you if you're stoned," I say.

"How about Rhodium?" he says. "That's a pretty name."

"What kind of name is that?" I say.

"It's the forty-fifth element on the periodic table," he says. "Let's name her after one of the earth's elements."

"Please," I say. "She is not a science experiment. This is not a science experiment, Jacob."

"Yes," he says. "No offense, but yes it is."

February 14

Eva. Your name is Eva. May you be as solid as tungsten steel, as essential as rhodium. You are made of all the elements: wind, heart, synapse; oh, Eva, let whatever you say be sane.

February 17

"What did you expect anyway?" says my sister. "Jacob is a great guy, but he's a *guy*."

"Meaning what?" I say.

"You know what I mean," she says. "The Y chromosome. It has its limitations."

"That's a stupid comment," I say, and then add, "no offense."

"Well," she says, "isn't it true that Y-carrying sperm swim faster but die earlier? Men don't have a lot of staying power."

"So what are you telling me? That I'm doomed to some horrible hetero arrangement where I care for the child and cook casseroles?"

"Sort of," she says.

"Jacob's a feminist," I say. "He'll catch on."

"Even if he does catch on," she says, "I think there's a limit. Fatherhood is something you do," she says. "Motherhood is something you are."

February 18

Essay idea: Write an essay challenging the premise of antenatal depression as a pure hormonal phenomenon. Could it not also be rooted in a woman's sense that she's in for a rapid decline in social status?

Scene: Eating lunch with editors two years ago. Editor of one magazine saying every woman who has a baby and goes part-time loses her edge in the job.

Crux: The paradox of the whole thing is that motherhood is the most powerful of all biological experiences and the most disempowering of all social ones.

February 19

I tell my boss, "I'm pregnant."

"You think I couldn't see?" she says. "You get three months maternity leave."

"Three months!" I say, I practically shout.

"What?" she says. "It's not enough? If you feel strongly about it, you can negotiate for six."

"Six months," I say, "I don't want six months. I don't want three months."

"How much do you want?" she asks.

"One week," I say.

My boss squints at me. "No woman," she says slowly, "has a baby and takes *one week* off from work."

I hear, then, a ringing inside my ear, a high little silver bell shivering fast.

"No woman," I say, "except me."

"What about the baby?" my boss says.

"I'll love her better," I say, "if I know I can leave her."

"You'll change your mind," my boss says. "As soon as she comes you're going to fall so much in love with her. It's a given. Who knows, you might decide you don't want to come back to work at all."

"Never," I say.

"Never say never," she says. She offers me a chocolate Kiss from the candy bowl on her desk. I accept. I unwrap the foil, pull out the paper strip, hold the dark pucker on my palm. I put it in my mouth and it is almost an ache, how strong the chocolate is, this sweet smear stinging my throat, dripping down.

February 20

He is not coming around. My sister may be right. I picture this baby in everything I do. When I get into the car I think, *In four months I'll be getting into the car with a baby;* when I eat dinner I think, *A baby will be here, throwing carrots;* when I go to sleep I think, *A baby will be breathing in the room down the hall, and we'll hear it on the monitor;* I cannot escape the baby. He, on the other hand, the one who wanted the baby more than I, seems to have his eyes sewn shut. I price cribs, consider car seats, study the vast assortment of nipples in the drugstores—slow flow, medium, one hole, two hole—and meanwhile he has his eyes sewn shut. He brings home exotic plants and tends them for hours, red saguaro opening in our home. An *Arunda donax* grows six feet tall in the hall. The bigger my belly, the more intense his hobbies. Plants. Electricity. Sci-fi stories that he reads for hours, I pick them up. Here is a whole new world. Here, comets of diamond fling themselves through the sky. Hello, I call to him. Hello. Sometimes he looks scared. He does not answer.

February 26

I go for my twenty-fourth-week ultrasound. I'm partly nervous—all these medications I'm on raise the possibility of birth defects—and partly excited because I'll get to see her again. If I felt some kind of thin thread of a connection at the amnio, then surely now, as her bigger body comes into view, I'll feel a similar, incremental swelling in my own heart.

It's freezing out today. The city buildings glitter like cutlery, the scream of a siren, I walk into the hospital lobby.

This is the hospital where I'll have her, if we make it that far, in only four more months.

The transition time that pregnancy is is slowly coming to a close. The change will charge forth, here, complete. Is this why I feel so suddenly a terror descending? Or is it because of the impending ultrasound, a cleft lip, a club-foot, a clogged heart, all possibilities when a mother takes lithium, Prozac, Klonopin during gestation.

I ride the elevator up to the antenatal diagnostic center.

Inside, at the front desk, one woman takes my hospital card while a technician says to her, "Last night I had a dream all my teeth fell out."

"Well," the woman says, processing my card, "you're probably some sicko. Do you ever dream of snakes? Have a seat," she says to me, and I sit, and I think of teeth, bone, and protein, the little ridged edges, crooked now, crumbling now.

Then they take me into the ultrasound room. The technician who's had the dream of teeth squirts the goopy gelatinous stuff all over my belly, and we watch the monitor for the fetus to come into view.

"That's a foot," she says. "And there's the femur." The technician explains how the ultrasound can scan right through skin, right through skull, to show brain and heart, liver and lungs; the lobes come into view, and then we zoom upward, enter the baby's damp cortex. "All there," she says.

"That's good," I say.

Click click click goes the magical machine.

"Good feet," the technician says. "No clubfeet here. Your baby looks fine."

"That's good," I say again, although I feel oddly removed, desultory, no surge of relief; it is a bit like being told some distant acquaintance has healed well from surgery; I'm mildly glad, but entirely untouched.

Untouched, then, I lie and watch. I am waiting to see not the organs of this fetus we have come to call Eva but her body, her shape, what I will someday rock. I need at least the sight of her skin to wake me.

But, unlike the last time, Eva never comes clear, she just spins and churns, a white blur, *Eva*, I think, *some love*, I think, but she will not show herself to me.

"Where is she?" I say, and then, as if in answer to my question, her face makes a sudden, startling appearance; it is right there, pressed up against the camera's lens, not a baby's face, not a human face, it appears huge and haunted, cruel little lips, bulbous black eyes; it is like seeing the face of an ancestor from a past so shrouded and dim no words remain to tell its tale. I shrink back. "That's her?" I say.

The technician laughs. "They look weird at this stage," she says. "Just an hour ago I had a mother in here who said, 'Whatever you do, don't give me a picture of that.'"

Eva is playing with the camera. She recedes back into swirls, then jumps forth again, her huge oval eyes, her mouth clenched closed; she claws at something and, then, the impossible happens. She opens her mouth. It is like seeing a black flower bloom. Her lips part and I know, suddenly know, absolutely, she is trying to speak. She is trying to tell me something. She is not a baby but an ancient with a wisdom so profound and paranormal that it will leave her mute and memoryless as soon as she is born. In the womb she has words, and she wants me to know what they are, and I see her strain and strain to pass some message through the membrane of my skin, but before I can come to clarity, come to Eva Claire, the technician clicks off and the screen goes blank and my belly is rubbed dry.

"You can get up now," she says and leaves the room.

I don't get up. I lie there, my pants unzipped, the monitor silent. Now I will not know. I will not know her or her words.

And when she is born, at the moment she becomes ensouled and secular, all her prenatal knowledge will vanish, the poems of water and gills and God knows what else, she will become a baby, then, at the moment she's born, and I'll have to teach her to talk the words she's lost; we'll start at the very beginning. "Here is a house," I will say, "here a seashell, here some sand, here a truck, here pink, here a heart."

My own heart is beating wildly, although what emotion drives it I cannot say. I am not detached anymore. I may be frightened.

I will try to remember you, Eva Claire, your real face, your true self, the story you so wanted to tell.

At some level, you are tied to the lizard's scales and the large glaciers. You know the sound of the earth as it evolves.

I am awed and humbled. I am terrified, lonely, moved, and impressed but still, still not in love.

February 27, 2:30 A.M.

This I don't understand. It's in the middle of a late winter night and I can't feel the baby move. I've lain awake for hours, prodding my stomach, changing positions, but there is no response. I think Eva has died. She was trying to tell me her time was near, that was the unsent message.

I lie awake. Next to me, Jacob snores peacefully, at my feet little Lila, draped and relaxed. I am not relaxed. I am rigid and waiting. *Move, Eva. Move,* I think. The intensity of my desire surprises me.

I watch the clock. The digital numbers flip, flip, flip, and then a cramping deep in my belly, a band tightening, something cinches and throbs. It is not the baby. It is blood.

My mouth goes dry. If she came out of me now, I suddenly realize, I would grieve.

Then I think I hear her. I think I feel her. A flutter.

Slowly it may be starting, this mother coming to care.

February 28

I love Sunday mornings at our house. Jacob and I drink coffee brewed with cinnamon and nutmeg, read the paper, the quiet of the neighborhood seeping into our kitchen, persisting throughout the day. So sweet.

Except today. Today, as we eat bagels and drink our coffee, Jacob says, "I've been thinking."

"What?" I say.

"We have so little time left," he says.

"You mean before the baby comes?" I say. "Or in life, in general."

"Both," he says, "but mostly before the baby."

I feel a twinge of fear, and also hope. I think he's starting to see.

"So little time," he says. "I'm going to really miss being in the house alone. I'm going to really miss the quiet."

"I know," I say. "It'll be so weird. There'll be Eva and probably a baby-sitter. Like right now, they would maybe both be in the kitchen with us. No privacy."

"Less privacy," he says, "but we'll get our lives back."

"You think?" I say.

"In ten years," he says, and what might be sadness, or terror, flits across his face. Jacob, after all, is a man of great quirkiness and solitude.

"Do you still want to have a baby?" I whisper.

"How much time do we have," he says, "till abortion becomes illegal?"

"After all we've been through," I say, my mouth dry, "you want to get an abortion?"

His face breaks into a playful smile. "Nah," he says, "we'll keep her."

"If she died," I say, "if she died in utero, would you feel sad?"

"Oh," he says, "yes. I'd feel great grief."

"Is that because you love her?" I say.

"I love her potential," he says. "She is all potential to me at this point."

"So you don't love her, actually," I say.

"How can I?" he says. "Right now, to me, she is just an idea that kicks."

March 4

We finally had sex. We were under the covers, reading. I poked him. "You want to have sex?" I said.

"Sure," he said, as though I were offering him a glass of water.

I'm not the only one who's become less desirous; so has he. He is, to be sure, always kind and admiring. He whooshes with admiration for my swelling belly. He marvels at the navel, which has risen up from its marsupial pouch, all knot and crease. He looks with interest at my breasts, the size of blowfish, latticed with veins. But he does all this with a distant, careful kind of attitude, as though the bigger I get, the more breakable I become.

Still, we had sex. The whole time I thought, *He's going to crush the baby.*

A long time seemed to pass. Eva grew very still. And then I felt a brief but painful ripping. He stopped, held me, rolled off.

Some people, at this point in the act, at the end of the act, reach for cigarettes, others wine or mooshu pork. I, however, immediately started grasping about on the floor for the stethoscope Jacob had bought a few weeks back, with which we liked to listen to the movements of the fetus.

"What are you doing?" he said as I geared up, holding the silver disc, plugging my ears. I moved the freezing circle around and around on my belly. All outer sounds ceased, and through the stethoscope's tubing traveled the mysterious blood-whooshings of the placenta, the watery thrums, the whole world dissolved, devolved, turned into this—here—now—this vascular, breathing mass.

I peered over at Jacob, who, understandably, may have looked a little insulted. I kissed my palm, placed it on his cheek, went back to my inner observations. Where was Eva? Had she survived? I searched for her heartbeat, for the sound of her fists or her knocking knees, just some sign, Eva, to let me know you're all right.

And then I heard her. Or it. Or something. Snoring. I heard Eva snoring—that's impossible, fetuses don't snore—but the sound was so distinct, so deep and amplified, the baby curled on her side, peacefully sucking her thumb, her watery exhalations rising in bubbles of rhythmic sound.

"Jacob," I whispered. "Jacob, hear this."

I turned to him, unplugged my ears, but he was fast asleep, satisfied snores rumbling through the twin tunnels of his nose; that was what I'd heard, of course.

For a long time, then, I listened to my husband's snores. I hate the word *husband*, because it means to plow a fertile field. I am not a field, nor is Jacob a plow. Well then, what were we, what was he, to me? A partner? That sounded like we were in business together. A companion? That evoked in me an image of a yellow Labrador retriever, a Seeing Eye dog in a harness. A friend, a lover, what would he become, what would happen—had already happened to our intimacy—with a baby between us?

Very carefully then, so as not to wake him, I placed the now warmed silver disc on his heart. Eva, as though on cue, started to stir inside me. I felt her kicks, heard his beats—is this what family is, this density of connection, this fibrous overlapping of skin, sound, fear, news, food? I listened for a while. I liked his sound combined with her movements, both inside me now, all inside me now, but I was glad, too, to take the stethoscope off, to sink into sleep, which came to me that night as a preciously private place, a black sea where I was me, alone.

March 5

I forget everything. I miss appointments, leave groceries to melt in the car, make lists and then misplace them, so these days, in my house, I come across random sheets of paper with tasks neatly numbered but never done. I have read that high levels of estrogen "cause" this absentmindedness. I picture it like this. Estrogen is not a liquid but a solid, sandpaper rubbing and rubbing the coiled cortex until the brain is smooth and stupid, a waxed bowling ball, heavy in the head.

One study shows pregnant women score ten points lower on IQ tests than they do in their nonpregnant states. At the same time, though, PET scans reveal the pregnant brain is like a lily pond, rich in proliferating axons and dendrites, green growths sprouting at a rate far faster and more ornate than at any other time in a person's life. It doesn't make sense, how the brain could be, anatomically speaking, far more baroquely wired in the gravid state and yet so much less capable of functioning.

This is what I think. Pregnant women are not dumber than their nonpregnant counterparts or their prior selves; rather, a new sort of intelligence is rising from the lobes. Short-term forgetfulness may clear the way for a deeper, more imaginative kind of cognition. Pregnancy, contrary to popular notions, may be the most cerebral time of a woman's life.

My mind is engaged all the time, so of course the details are that much harder to hang on to. Every moment of the day is taken up with the tiring task of composing a new life script, creating characters from scratch. In some moments, my daughter, Eva, has black hair and blue eyes. In other moments, I make her hands on me, damp hands full of germs, we both get sick.

Jacob is here. We are old now. Eva has gone to college, a pack of Marlboros in her pocket. She has curly hair, red, like her father's, and she is studying anthropology at the University of Massachusetts. Why the University of Massachusetts? Why don't I imagine my girl at Harvard? Who can interpret the mysteries of this script? "Don't smoke," I tell her.

And then she is on a horse.

And then she is in a crib.

And then she is making love with a man.

And then she is coming out of me, slick and screaming, her head an oiled plum.

I see our futures in multiple prismatic representations all day, every day, my mind aching from the effort, but I cannot stop. I am like the girl in the red shoes; the pregnant brain dances on and on, through the thickets and over the groves, relentless, Botticellian, Scheherazadian, spinning the strangest of daily tales.

March 12

Jacob has made a new friend. He met her, he says, in Harvard Square. Her name is Amanda, and she has several colors in her hair. She makes mobiles out of tire parts. "Out of *tire parts?*" I say. "Don't be so closed-minded," he says. "She's very gifted."

"Has she ever sold anything?" I ask. I'm being catty.

Some nights, Amanda comes over and drinks tea. Other nights, though, he goes to her studio. He comes home smelling of rubber.

March 17

Men do desert pregnant women. They are also unfaithful to them. . . . Since, reproductively, they have nothing tangible to gain from intercourse with her, natural selection has so fashioned their aesthetics that they respond with less sexual interest to the shape of a pregnant woman than to a non-pregnant one. . . . Men have been programmed to show greatest sexual interest in

the female body with a waist measuring about 70 per cent of the
circumference of her hips.

Robin Baker, *Baby Wars*

I'm just about to leave for Washington, a two-day conference where I'll be presenting on the ethics of what's
called cosmetic psychopharmacology. I'm here in my office at work, small bag packed by my side, and I suddenly
remember I need to tell Jacob to leave the door unlocked
tomorrow morning, so the men who have come to refinish
our floors can get in to complete the job. I call him at his
chemistry company.

"I'm sorry," the receptionist says. "He's left for the day."

Three forty-five. Left for the day? Since when does Jacob leave work early? He never gets home before eight at
night. I call home.

I get no answer. For some reason, a strange anxiety
fills my fingers, my arms and legs. I ring back his company. "I'm sorry," I say to the receptionist, "but I really
need to speak to him. Did he tell you where he was
going?"

"No," she says, and I picture him in a car, driving with
Amanda, or another lover I have never, and at the same
time always, known about.

No sex. His lack of interest. My lack of interest. His
sci-fi books and distance. The evolutionary biology book
I've been reading, which talks about the likelihood of men
straying during pregnancy. And his own father, I suddenly
remember him telling me, who left his mother when she

was pregnant with her second child. Of course. It all comes together.

"I need," I say to the receptionist, "to get a message to him," and indeed this is true, for we share a house where the floors are being finished, and he must leave the door unlocked by 11:00 A.M. tomorrow.

"Well," she says, "I can e-mail a message, and when he comes back in, he'll get it."

"I'm going out of town," I say. "I need to make sure he gets the message before eleven tomorrow morning," I say.

"That," she says, "might be a little difficult. When he left he said he wouldn't be in the office all day tomorrow."

"All day?" I say.

"I hope," she says, "that I am not getting myself in the middle of something."

We hang up. I try him at our house again. Still no answer. The suspicion is becoming certainty. I have three hours before my plane leaves. I drive home. I don't know why, but I suddenly, definitely, have to go home.

Inside the floors, newly coated, have a hysterical shine. Sunlight bounces off them. The dogs are gone, off at the kennel where they stay when I go away, but I find pieces of them, their copper hairs on the stairs, that's all. "Hello?" I call. Who, exactly, do I expect to answer? And if he is here, what, exactly, do I expect to find? Another woman on a mattress in his study? Jacob is a man of mystery, of secrets, which is why I love him, and can never completely trust him.

I climb the stairs. The door to his study is partway

open, and some sunlight slips through. I feel a tongue of fresh air from an open window lift the hem of my skirt. I hear a rustling sound, something shuffling and muffled, and I push open the door to find it; I push it hard and angry, so the sight is sudden and complete.

And this, this is what I see. Nothing. Or everything, the jumbled chaos that constitutes the singular life of the man I love. Molecules made from toothpicks and marshmallows hang from the ceiling. Since I've been pregnant, he's made estrogen, progesterone, and relaxin, and I see them now, slender wooden sticks joined by candied puffs, replica of my body, swaying in the breeze in my lover's room. But the lover himself? I look left, right. Not here. Chemistry books are stacked high beside his desk, big, heavy books with bright orange covers, magnified cells that look like suns, fiery rays shooting out from the molten nuclei.

I step back. I walk further down the hallway, tiptoeing practically, like I am a thief in a foreign house, like home is nowhere near.

In what will be the baby's room, the white crib stands in utter sunlight. The windows have no shades yet; the yellow walls are alive.

I go over to the window that looks toward our backyard. The heaviness in my gut is not all fetus. Something is wrong with our marriage; he is having an affair and, in a way, I cannot blame him.

For a long time I stand looking out that window. I think I will miss my plane. I think I don't care. I see a shadow move across the window in the gardening hut by the back fence. I peer closer. And then I go down.

The smells are astounding. The scent of fresh sliced orange. The tropical coconut, which I see in white rings on the platter my grandmother gave us. What must be coconut milk sits in a clear glass, a watery, slightly oily substance. I have drunk it before, as a small child in the Caribbean, a man holding a husk to my lips, the taste of sweet nut, like mother's milk perhaps, here it is. When I open the door to the gardening shed I find him, milk in hand, flagrant strawberries piled high in a bowl and, beside that, a hunk of black pumpernickel bread. He is alone.

"What are you doing?" I say to him. I feel the tension break in me, relief and tears and questions, for here he is, I have found him, he is alone and I still have no idea.

He looks at me. He puts down his glass of tropical milk. He picks up a strawberry and bites into its seeded side. The strawberry is as red as his tongue, both blend, man and fruit. "What are *you* doing?" he says to me, chewing thoughtfully. "I thought you were going to Washington."

I take in more of the scene. The floor of the gardening shed is sprinkled with dirt; cobwebs are in every corner, but he has set the table. I see cheese, a yellow wedge.

"Are you having an affair?" I say, and the tears come fast now, fast and loose.

He looks at me, a little puzzled. He looks around him, at the scene he's set. "No," he says. "I'm having a snack."

"That's some snack," I say, "in the middle of a workday, and the receptionist told me you're not coming in tomorrow. What's going on?"

He shrugs, palms up. "You're going to Washington," he says. "The dogs are gone. We're having a baby. I thought I'd take advantage of what might be my last time alone at home. That's it," he says. "That's all."

I stare at him. I stare and stare, for this is very odd, this tropical party for one. "What are you doing in the gardening shed?" I say. "Why the gardening shed?"

"The smell of polyurethane on the floors," he says, "lethal stuff. I didn't want to breathe it, and, really, neither should you. You shouldn't even be anywhere near this house with the floors still wet."

"I thought you were having an affair," I say. I weep, and then it occurs to me he is. He's having an affair with himself or, more accurately, toasting the end of his lifelong affair with himself. He feels the changes pressing in. He is saddened and celebratory, both. For the first time, I see what fatherhood might mean.

"Why," he says, "would I have an affair, when I have you and Eva and the dogs?"

"What about Amanda?" I say.

"Tire parts?" he says, and laughs. "Come on," he says, "she's a friend. She's not my type."

"I read this book," I say, and I try to explain to him about hip-to-waist ratio, but he interrupts.

"Join me?" he offers, holding out some coconut, tearing off a slice of the black bread. I sit with him. He leans forward, kisses my cheek. In just a few more hours, I will be the one to fly away. But for now, I sit with him. We say nothing. We feel sacred, and together, and apart and changing, all, all at once. We pass the platters back and forth between us, sampling this strange, new food.

RELAXIN

Why contraction? It is less a spasm and more an opening. The tiny porthole of the vagina expands to ten times its normal size during delivery; the pinpoint os of the cervix widens enough for a fist, and then a head. The human infant's head is roughly eight inches in diameter, a miniature but mighty planet; the mother's pelvis, on the other hand, is significantly smaller than that. This puts our species in a difficult conundrum, a camel through the eye of a needle, birth as a Christian paradox. In other species, the infant heads are smaller, because, of course, the brains are smaller; in exchange for our intelligence we get a treacherous descent.

Plus we get relaxin, one of the least-understood chemicals in the female body. It is a hormone—hormona, from the Greek root "to change, to instigate," which relaxin certainly does—but, unlike estrogen and progesterone, which circulate in the blood all through the female life cycle, relaxin is purely pregnancy specific. It has a lovely name: Re-lax-in, like a yawn, like a hammock on a day in mid-July. Indeed, relaxin is a loosener, a tissue softener, its subtle, continuous pulses from the third trimester on causing the collagen fibers in the cervix to thin and expand, causing the flesh of the vaginal walls to give up their tone so they can stretch like a piece of pink spandex. Relaxin acts on the bony joints as well; like a lubricant, it gets into calcified cracks between knuckles, toes, the white handles of a woman's hips, which, in childbirth, must rip right out of their stone and ball sockets so the skull can pass through.

Without relaxin, birth would not be possible. In one study, scientists engineered relaxin-free rats, got them pregnant, and waited to see what would happen. The rat pups both developed and died in utero, all curled up there, seven sailors stuck in a rigid ship. By the twenty-sixth week of pregnancy, assuming relaxin levels are normal, your uterus and cervix are the antithesis of rigid; they are marvelous, silky, milky textiles, outrageous stretchy satin in deep merlot colors; you are young again. This is a literal as well as a figurative truth. Relaxin as an elixir is being investigated by cosmetic companies to give the face and breasts that baby softness, that line-free look; it is under consideration for fibromyalgia treatment as well; rub it there, right on the inexplicable ache, and some sort of soothing occurs. As for you, in the third trimester, you are at once bulky and lithe, how strange. You can barely roll over in bed but, if you tried, you could do a clean, knifelike split. You are greased, a body bendable, a woman in motion, even while you wait, feeling the kicks, sitting very still.

THE THIRD TRIMESTER

March 20

Third trimester. I go to the lab to get my medication levels checked. There is me, wonderfully sane for now, and then there is Eva, who every night soaks in the salt of lithium and other pills. Behind all my marital anxieties, beneath all my pleasures, there is always this question, this image—my daughter in the Dead Sea, a place of too much salt, ragged mountains surrounding her briny body.

So I go to the lab. I sit in a dentist's chair while a technician takes tube after tube of blood. On a bookshelf sits a notebook—"Bridgewater State Hospital for the Criminally Insane" I read on its binder.

"What's that?" I say, nodding toward the notebook.

"That," she says, "is to keep track of the criminals' blood work. We do a lot of criminals here."

"I see," I say. When she leaves the room I look at all the tubes of fresh fluid, mine and others'. *Here*, I think, *is the blood from a murderer, here from a thief, here from me.* What separates us, really? We have all acted out of madness, put others at risk for the sake of our own salvations.

I pick up a vial, and when I shake it a thin sediment coats the walls of the glass. Fetal cells, I have read, circulate in a mother's blood long, long after the baby is born. Scientists have found fetal cells in sixty-, seventy-year-old females. A woman carries the bodies of every baby she has ever borne for the rest of her life; she is imprinted. She is imprisoned in the memory, guilt, and gladness, sitting always side by side. That's the difference. The real criminal dismisses his crime; but the mother, she is inscripted, a literal, cellular conscience.

I care.

March 24

We are lying in bed, early morning. "My blood levels came back normal," I say to him. "Now let's just hope the baby's normal too."

"She'll be an interesting mixture of chemicals," Jacob says. "Quite an experiment."

"Look," I say, defensive. "A lot of babies have been born to mothers who have taken the drugs I'm on. The babies are usually fine."

"I know," he says, "but consider my contribution. I've been working in chemistry labs for years, absorbing all those toxins. Who knows what's happened to my DNA."

"So she'll be born with flippers," I say.

"I'd rather wings," he says. "Quick, get the nets, she just flew over the delivery table, she's heading down to X Ray, radio ahead . . ."

We start to laugh, we contract together, it feels good, how much we laugh, how hard and urgent while the black bats fly above.

And yet, I cannot see the bats. As far as I know my daughter does not have wings, and my mind is still intact. We get up. It is Wednesday. The sound of the church bells is remarkably clear. Outside, children ride red bicycles, a policeman holds up a white-gloved hand, and all the traffic stops.

Jacob goes to work. I go to Tara's house. Tara, whom I have never met before, is a new patient with such severe agoraphobia she claims she must be seen at home. The Department of Social Services is threatening to remove her children because of an alcohol problem leading to child abuse.

It takes me over an hour to get there. She lives at the very rim of the city, where skyscraper and ocean meet in a tide of grit.

I am always amazed at how, when the mind is clear, when the mood is good, even the ugliest scenes can seem lovely. This, perhaps, is the danger of health, of happiness, for when I look out my car window at the passing poverty, at the old pouchy men on the seawall, at the bikers in black trading packets of heroin, I perceive an almost romantic Bukowskian poetry to it all, the smells and sights, I on an adventure, the way my mood removes me and relieves me of responsibility for the social hardships all around me. Some claim that depressed individuals have, in fact, a more realistic view of the world; it could be true. It could comfort me when I think of what lies ahead. But I don't think about what lies ahead. I speed down the road, ballooned along on my big belly and the sea winds and the salsa music in the air.

Tara lives in a tenement. The road is so narrow my truck won't fit. I have to pee in the urgent, burning way of the pregnant woman. Lately my bladder, not my mind, has been the biggest focal point. I think about my bladder all the time. It is a muscular bottle, a blue bowl that passively fills, and fills, as the fluids of fecundity travel down, and in. My bladder is a lake. My bladder aches. My sphincter, that gorgeous ring of pinkish tissue, opens at its urging, and the hot release jets forth. This is what I have become, in the third trimester. A bladder, and I love it. I love it so long as I am home, and near the bathroom, where I can repeat the ritual of release and relief as often as I need.

Now, however, I am not home. I am about to meet a patient. The unfortunate side to the bladder story is this. If I do not give my bladder, which is like a wild horse, its head, it will buck and run off all on its own. Let me put this less poetically. No matter how many Kegels I do, I have started to pee in my pants. I don't mind peeing in my pants, except when there's a patient involved. So Eva disappears. Jacob disappears. The world disappears as I slosh over to the doorway, ring the buzzer, my sphincter squeezed shut.

"Dr. Slater," I say, holding out my hand when a short, stocky woman answers. "Lauren Slater. Are you Tara?"

"Yeah," she says, and we move into the darkness of her apartment, cinder-block walls, a cigarette twinkling like an ulcer at the corner of her lip.

She looks at my stomach, puts out her cigarette, which I appreciate. Nevertheless, what with the smell of smoke in the air, I cough and a little jet of urine spurts out.

"Would you mind," I say, "if I use your bathroom?"

This, I know, is not the optimal way to begin a thera-peutic relationship, but when the bladder speaks, it is like a call from God.

"Well," she says, "I don't have any toilet paper. I'm all out."

"That's okay," I say, smiling desperately now, for the lit-tle leak is growing more vigorous, drop by fat drop. "That's okay. I can use a paper towel."

"Shit," she says, "I don't have any paper towels either." She goes to her cabinets, flings them open. Inside I see bottles upon bottles of Scotch and vodka, a bong gone gray with smoke, and a mirror with white dust still on it. I see, also, as her sleeves slide up, a tattoo of a snake curled around a cross, a pirate puffing on a pipe. Tara denies having a substance abuse problem, but my bladder-driven method of evaluation seems to be suggesting otherwise.

"No," she says, "no towels here."

"A napkin?" I say, my voice now small and high and hopeful.

Tara sighs, turns her palms up.

"Oh that's okay," I say hurriedly. "Look, forget it, I don't need any paper products, I'll just, I'll just," I want to say "drip dry," but I can practically hear the collective groan of every supervisor I've ever had.

"I've got it," Tara says, snapping her fingers in the air. She rushes to a small balcony, flings open the screen. The tenements across the way are so close we could touch them. "Hey, Donna," she shouts out, hands cupped around her mouth. Everyone on the thronging street below stops what they're doing, looks up. "Hey, Donna, my psychiatrist is here, and she's pregnant, and she's really gotta go. You have any toilet paper over there?"

I never actually see Donna, but after a few moments two rolls of toilet paper get lobbed into the air, one after the other, silently. The first one Tara catches. The second one bounces off the railing and streams into the street.

"One outta two," Tara says, handing me a roll. I clutch it. I look over her railing. Down below the children are screaming with delight, giddy as they wrap themselves in the softest streamers, each one pure white, a present, they twirl and twirl in this monotone maypole. *Remember this*, I say to myself. *Appreciate this*, I say to myself, and truly I do, each child a well-wrapped gift, and then my body, all water and rush.

March 25

Each day now the movements are growing stronger. The third trimester, it seems to me, has less to do, at least so far, with marital difficulties or bonding concerns, and more to do with preparation for the impending physical event. It's not that the other worries have vanished, but I seem to be experiencing them more remotely. I don't think so much about my marriage, or even the baby. Instead, my mind is on this: I have about three months to go and my Kegels sag, my lower back aches, my heart is inefficient. I've started working out, following the lessons outlined in a book called *The Tuppler Technique: Exercise for Maternal Fitness*. According to Ms. Tuppler, a pregnant woman should do over one hundred Kegels a day. You should, she says, visualize a penny at the entrance to your vagina. Visualize your vaginal lips picking the penny up, drawing it in, and in, until it reaches your cervix, then the tip of your uterus, then your navel, at which point you push the penny back out—*release* is the key word here—your cervix unfolding, so says Ms. Tuppler, like a flower.

So today I am sitting cross-legged in my bedroom, picking up pennies with my genitals, vaginally inhaling copper and then expelling in a motion at once forceful and flowery. This is ridiculous. I don't like Ms. Tuppler's images. I don't like the thought of a penny inside me, or the thought of my labia, like some Venus flytrap reaching out for riches.

Sixty years ago Virginia Woolf wrote about the difficulties women have in articulating their own flesh. Since that time the women's movement has come, and gone, and come again; there are far fewer angels in the house, and yet her stance still stands, alarmingly, contemporarily, correct. We have no good poetics of the female body, at least in the mainstream culture, and the language of pregnancy and birth underscores this. When I'm lying like a trussed chicken and the doctor is in me to his elbow, or when I'm squatting, bare-assed and panting, I want a way of imaging myself that is neither shameful nor silly, if only to preserve my own dignity. There is no dignity in catching pennies. And I will not be sweetened like a stupid bloom. I want words that are proud and intelligent, a handsome language of arch and flex.

March 31

The first night of Passover, and somewhere, far across the country in a state whose name I do not even know, my mother is setting the table. She is laying a soft white cloth over dark mahogany; she is bringing out the Pesach platter—shank bone, egg, horseradish. I know her movements, having watched them throughout my childhood; no matter how much distance and distress there is between us, I cannot forget her. I call her.

"It's Lauren," I say. We have not spoken in months and months. My mother has much contempt for me; this is nothing new.

"I know," she says. Her voice crisp and curt.

"Happy Passover," I say.

"Well it won't be," she says, she spits, "but good of you to call."

I'm sitting on my unmade bed, a place rumpled and

warm. I can hear Jacob in his study, the slow shuffle of turning pages. *I have a home here*, I think, *this is where I live now*, but her bitterness, the worm in my mother's heart, never fails to unnerve me.

"So," I say, all forceful energy, "how's your winter been?"

"Nice of you to ask," she says. "Terrible. And you?"

"You know I'm pregnant," I say, and then—what else?—tears flush out my eyes.

"You think only of yourself," she says.

In her voice I hear the familiar sound of rage, the origins of which I have never understood—a biochemical mishap, a hidden trauma, a rape? I often think my mother was raped. What else could account for the hard dots of hatred in her eyes?

I touch my stomach, where it peaks. "I'm over seven months," I say. "I'm getting pretty big."

"All I need," she says, "is some appreciation. I am the whipping boy, the doormat. And who is here to help me out?"

"I'm going to hang up now, Mom," I say, my voice soft, for I have long ago learned there is no use tussling with her. Soon, I know, my stepfather will come to comfort her. She has married a rich man. Servants will dust her shelves, draw her bath, and in the night, when no one can hear, maybe the softer side will emerge, and she will weep for things I cannot ever understand—her secrets, a lost dove, a park bench, a penny.

I replace the receiver. "Well, Eva," I say, looking down at the bulge, but I cannot finish my sentence. I really have nothing to say. Eva will have no grandmother, as I had no mother, as my mother had no mother, and so on down, and so on back, through time.

"Well the buck stops here," Jacob says, when I repeat the conversation. "No more hatred in this generation."

But, of course, I worry. I worry about so much but, mostly, I worry about the worm, that it is in me, too.

April 9

I am so joyful today. I am so full of expectation. Forget my mother. Forget it all. It is April, and the light is lengthening, and I am paddling in the mysteries of the sweetest mood. Soon I will have a daughter. This must mean my body works, I am a part of evolution, I am included. I cannot wait to hold her.

April 11

Our first childbirth class. There are seven other couples, plus the instructor, who makes us sit on the floor to promote healthy circulation. Immediately I feel resentful. I have no interest in sitting on the floor, especially when, to the left of me, there's a nice big couch that just begs for a body, a bowl of nachos, and some salsa.

"You should make sure you eat a hundred grams of protein a day," the instructor says to us. I look over at Jacob and mouth *a hundred grams?* I'd have to consume an entire turkey. Jacob shrugs.

"Every day is an opportunity for you to help your baby grow," she says. "Think of *each little thing* you put in your mouth."

I look around at the other class participants. They are all nodding appreciatively. They are, also, very, very fat. It is difficult to tell, in fact, whether or not the women are actually pregnant or just overweight. Or maybe I'm not being fair. Maybe I'm being bitter. There's the worm.

"Fruits, vegetables, liver, meats, and no drugs. *No drugs,*" the instructor repeats.

I bite my lip, look down.

"Our philosophy is that a woman should take *no drugs* during gestation and that she needs *no drugs* during labor and delivery. Think of animals. Do they need drugs? No. Do they pant and hyperventilate when giving birth? No. Birth, in nature, is a quiet, inward affair, and you are here to learn to replicate this in your own delivery experience."

A young woman raises her hand.

"Yes?" the instructor says.

"I agree with you," she says. "The problem is that we, in our society, don't live close enough to our instincts. If we did, we would all be able to have peaceful births and breast-feeding experiences."

All the other couples nod. *You brownnosing little dingdong,* I think. *You want to live close to your instincts? You want to roll in the mud like a pig? You want to give up your car and that silk pantsuit you're wearing?*

Why this worm? I say to myself.

I picture myself, every day, chugging down my Prozac with a glass of 2 percent. The lithium at night. I have to hate them, you see, before they can hate me.

"You're right," says the instructor. "How many of you are planning on breast feeding?"

Everyone but guess who raises her hand. I cannot breast-feed. Lithium taints the milk.

"Very good," says the instructor. "Breast is best. Anyone who plans to bottle-feed, well, I have nothing to say to them. I know nothing about it."

I look away, toward the window, where I can see a tiny patch of purpling sky. *Out there,* I think, and that comforts me.

"Now," says the instructor, her voice pulling me back, "I want you all to think of your responses to pain, physical or emotional." She takes out a whiteboard, a thick red marker.

"Visualization," someone says. She writes it down.

"Imagery," someone else offers.

"Crying."

"Distraction."

"Swearing."

"Focus."

"Panic," I say.

When we are done, she reads the list back to us. "Visualization," she says, "is an excellent way to deal with the pain of labor. Imagine you are on a sandy beach. . . . Or, if that doesn't work for you, crying is fine too. Distraction," she says, "is a technique a little less effective, but if it works, go with it, and swearing," she says, "well some women just need to swear to get through the contractions, and you should let yourself go with this, feel free, by all means. And panic," she says. She stops. "Who said panic?"

I tentatively poke my pencil into the air. She turns to me. "Do you really think," she says, "that panic is an adaptive way of dealing with pain?"

"But you didn't ask us," I say, and I'm genuinely confused, "you didn't ask us what were adaptive ways of dealing with pain. I just gave you an honest answer. My response to pain is often panic. In fact," I say, and I feel some glee rise in me, "my response to life is really often panic."

"Well," says the instructor, and I'm glad to see I've thrown her off her little lit-up boat, "we're just going to cross panic right off our list. What else," she says, "might you do with the pain of labor other than panic?"

"Actually," I say, "the labor pains don't really panic me that much." What do panic me, and what I don't tell her, are the brain pains, the synaptic collapses. "Labor," I continue, "has a definitive ending to it, so I'll use that knowledge to help me through. I mean, no matter what, you know it's going to be over, even if you're dead at the end. It will end."

Some of the other couples laugh. The instructor raises her eyebrows. "Yes," she says, "it does end. But you don't die. Of course you don't die."

"Statistics show," I say, "that two percent of women do

die as a result of labor-related complications. I think it's important to acknowledge that. I think it's important to be honest about this whole—" I stop. Everyone is staring at me. The statistic I have completely invented. Jacob puts his hand on my shoulder.

"Actually," I say, continuing, perseverating really, because I cannot stop now, some force pushes me forward, "actually I know someone who died during labor. She had massive hemorrhaging."

Where this story comes from I am not sure. Like the statistic, it is completely untrue, but I suddenly see this woman perfectly. Her name is Leanne. Her tombstone rises above the rest, into a gray day.

"That's an anomaly," the instructor says.

"I know someone," another person pipes up, "who didn't die, but who had a stroke when the doctor gave her an epidural."

"Terrible," I say.

"You know," says someone else, "that's why epidurals scare me. But I'll tell you what I'm really not looking forward to. I've heard"—and she lowers her voice—"that an episiotomy is worse than the labor itself."

"You have to sit on an inflatable donut for six weeks," a voice from the corner says.

"And when you, you know, have a bowel movement," a woman whose name tag reads Tanya offers, "sometimes the stitches split. Your urine burns like hell."

The instructor looks alarmed, but we're on a roll now, and I feel proud.

April 14

In my own, private millennium, time is hurtling forward. Less than *twelve weeks*. Time is tactile, visual. I see it whirring on its high-speed wheels, a silver train on mercuric tracks, it blurs by, all digital and sleek. I cannot stop time. People say that toward pregnancy's end, time slows down as boredom, and weight, set in, but not so for me. I am speeding through space, rounding corner after corner, making curtains, making bumpers, we need clothes, we need to kiss our single selves good-bye, this is time. Jacob feels it too. He is working ten, twelve, now fifteen hours a day. We walk around with a slightly startled look to our eyes. We speed up, keys clacking in our backs, two toys overdosed on Duracell. I must, while there is still time, read everything, write everything, talk to friends, savor the spring, plant hops, stay up lounging until dawn is in the sky. I do not dream of the baby. I dream of trains, I dream digital, I dream I am running or, rather, the road is running and I am on it and the scenery streaks by— European castles, Irish wars, and then swords hanging in the suddenly still air.

April 17

After work Jacob spends time on his computer, constructing and researching his family tree. "Who were your grandparents' parents?" he asks me. I cannot say. I am quintessentially American, self-constructed, sprung from foam and steel. My background is mysterious, my mother plagued by misery no one can name, my father oddly absent, living in some gated mansion at the very tip of Florida. At the age of ten my brother went to boarding school, as did my two sisters, and I went to live with a foster family, so I really have little idea about my origins. "You have to find out," Jacob says to me. "What are we going to tell Eva about her history?"

I am not sure about this. Often I think I have no need for history. It's an outdated concept, a Freudian construction, the idea that where you came from explains and dignifies who you currently are. I am who I am because of serotonin, because of norepinephrine, because dopamine courses in rich, dark deluges through my brain. I am who I am because billions of cells click and stutter, thus giving rise to this chemical yet utterly invisible thing we call imagination, and my imagination, which floats above my head like a cartoon bubble, but no, more beautiful than that, like the bubbles blown from soap and wand, my imagination creates and constructs, and every construct is true. Therefore, a woman named Leanne died giving birth, and her tombstone rises above the rest, into a gray day. My mother was a trapeze artist; she leapt from bar to bar. I tell myself these stories every day, my history manufactured from the dense physiology where spirit and gray matter meet; I have no need for history. I come from everywhere. I come from nowhere. I am radically free. I am empty.

But Jacob persists. Funny, how he is the chemist and yet clings to this traditional notion of history as a means of self-definition. Jacob can trace his family back through Germany, into the seventeenth century. "You should find out everything you can," he tells me, and keeps telling me, until at last I call my mother's parents, my maternal grandparents, and set up an appointment to see them.

I rarely see them—all the estrangement and silences—but tonight, the end of Shabbat, a clear Saturday in late April when the stars salt the sky, tonight I go. Their house is only twenty minutes from mine. As I enter the kitchen, the smell of my childhood comes back to me, the musty and precise odor of old leather, tarnished silver, fumes. "Lauren dear," my grandmother says, and cups my chin, kisses my cheek. I dislike her lips on me. She is so old, my grandmother, my mother's mother. I am suspicious of her. "What did you do to my mother?" I have often wanted to say but won't, can't; quiet, that is who we are.

And she is so old now, and the oldness is an ache, a burden that brings sadness to me. She is wearing a peach velour bathrobe, tattered slippers, all decay except her hair, a bright, fresh white.

We go to the den, take our seats. Upstairs my grandfather, who has suffered a stroke, lies mute in his hospital bed. Equipment clutters the house—wheelchairs, oxygen tanks—and then the shuffling feet of their twenty-four-hour nurse as she walks by.

"Grandma," I say, and I already hear defeat in my voice, for I expect nothing of her, I know nothing of her, except that she has dedicated her life to preserving surfaces. Cellophane wrappings still cover the pleated lampshades, a way of stopping dust, stopping time.

"I miss you, Lauren dear," my grandmother says to me, her voice raspy and worn; that she cannot hide, how age has taken her. "I wish you'd come see us more often. I wish you would come to family gatherings. Why weren't you at Thanksgiving?"

"Grandma," I say, "you know my mother doesn't invite me to her holidays. I was at my own home on Thanksgiving, with Jacob."

"All you need," she says, "is to apologize to your mother. A child owes her parents an apology. It's always up to the child—"

"Grandma," I say sharply. "I didn't come here to talk about this."

A silence falls between us. Her eyes get foggy, two windows when they've been breathed on. "All right," she finally says, "then tell me what you came here for."

I look at her, startled. Such a direct request. Such a sudden, gravelly force to her voice. When she shifts in her seat, the peach bathrobe falls away to reveal a grossly swollen leg, the mashed purple grapes of her varicose veins, and then, on her calf, a black gash.

"What happened to your leg?" I ask.

"When you are old," she says, "like I am, a lot of things change. My leg hurts," she says, "and I am on antibiotics. Yesterday, the nurse broke one of my favorite plates and, you know what, I didn't care. When I was younger I

would have cared, but what does a plate matter in life?"
She smiles. "I didn't care," she says again, and now I see
how age has opened her, and I swim in.

"So what do you care about now?" I ask. "Now that the
plates are gone."

"Time," she says, and that is when I notice it; how could
I have missed it before? The room is filled with clocks—
cuckoos, electric whirrings. Time is sensual. Time is not a
concept. It is a force. It is flesh.

"Grandma," I say, and I feel a tightness in my throat.
"Will you come see my daughter when she's born? You
know my mother won't. We can't deny it, Grandma. But
will you?"

"If I have to walk there," she says, "I will do it."

We sit in silence for a while. I am full of gratefulness. I
am no longer repelled. No amount of construct can replace the material truth. I have a grandmother. Her name
is Frances. Here, here is my history.

"When I was pregnant with your mother," my grandmother says, and then she tilts her head back, laughs. "Oh
my God," she says, "what a terrible time."

I laugh too, the excitement of honesty.

"At the birth," she says, "they put me into a twilight
sleep." And then my reticent, proper grandmother, lubricated by the specter of death, goes on to tell me how they
shot her full of a potent cocktail, so all the world swarmed
and through a sweaty scrim she could hear the screams
of other animals—or were they women?—pushing their
bloody loads into the world. Her memory went down,

came back, flickered. She felt a tearing, the cold claws of forceps as they pried my mother from her pouch. "I saw your mother then," my grandmother says, "all blue and smashed. It was not a pretty sight."

"And after the birth?" I ask. "What did you do, what did you feel right after the birth?"

"Oh my goodness," says my grandmother. "I was exhausted. You will be too. I turned over and went right to sleep."

And then she told me how the next morning, when she awoke, a nurse named Miss Tiebot was standing over her bed, holding out the baby. And Miss Tiebot said to my grandmother, "You missed your four A.M. feeding," and my grandmother said, "I'm tired, I want to still sleep," and Miss Tiebot said, "Don't you love your daughter?"

"When she asked me that," my grandmother said, a mischievous smile on her lips, "I considered it carefully. I thought for a moment and then I said, 'Yes, Miss Tiebot, I love my daughter, but I also love my sleep.'

"I never held her," my grandmother says now. She shrugs. "Not for months did I hold her. I didn't know how. No one ever told me. I thought she would break. My God," my grandmother says, a strange, strained laughter erupting, "my God, I'm surprised she came out normal."

"Grandma," I say, "Grandma, listen. My mother's not normal."

By the time I drive home, it's near midnight. We have talked for hours. "Who," I had asked before I left, "who was your mother, your mother's mother, and so on down the line?"

And now I know. I have the piece of paper in my coat pocket. Her mother's name was Sara, from Kiev, her grandmother Leah, also from Kiev, Leah's mother Mindle, from Russia. *Mindle,* I think to myself. What a wonderful name. It is not a name I could have made up. It is too particular, too *real,* Mindle. I feel absurdly proud. Mindle lived in a shtetl. Mindle, according to my grandmother, was a seamstress; there she is, her needle darting in and out of fabric. Mindle made dresses, prayer shawls, had spools of every color. I must believe she was kind.

And with me now there is Mindle, Leah, Sara, Frances, my grandmother. Before I left I helped my grandmother bathe her wounded leg, and the task was unspeakably precious to me. Warm water, a blue basin, a sponge cloth, the old blackened blood flaking away and rich crimson bubbles rising up. "It won't scab," my grandmother had said. "My blood is thin now," and thin it was, running down my fingertips, packed with heart and history.

And I am speeding in my truck now, the green signs bright in the spotlighted night. I wrapped her leg in gauze. I smelled her skin, half sweet, half rot. She blessed my head, laying her hands upon the fontanel like a rabbi, she closed her eyes. She blessed me without intent or even knowledge, but I felt, for sure, a prayer come through my grandmother's hands, a language of pulse and palm lines, and the prayer said this: May you hold her, and in holding her, hold us, forever down the line.

April 23

I'm in Cleveland tonight, in a posh hotel, it's pouring rain, and I rush to get dressed before the lecture I'm due to give in under half an hour. Cleveland State has asked me to speak on *Prozac Diary*, my book. The truth is, I have not at all prepared for this lecture. Too busy. Too busy. Not even a scribbled note. I strip off my leggings, my oversize shirt, and struggle my way into some tights. Hormones have changed my skin, so a taupe line plunges like an arrow from my navel to my pubis, and then, in the other direction, from my navel to my heart. Both my ambivalence and my readiness are written on my body. I am halved, marked like perforated paper. Touch me and I'll tear.

A car comes, takes me to the lecture hall. I roll in, approach the podium, everyone is watching. One hundred, two hundred people; this is not what they expected, I'm sure. When you think of an author, you think of someone tall and slim, someone who wears dark blazers and smokes a long cigarette. You think of expatriates, Hemingway's hard-boiled eggs, the drunken elegance of a Fitzgerald flapper, or the austere beauty of the Bloomsbury group. You do not think of this, a squat, rolling woman in a poorly patched dress, the face of a teenager, the body of earth.

"So," I say, all improvisation. "I am here to talk about autobiography," and then I'm off. I'm off on estrogen, relaxed on progesterone, heightened and ruddy; my words spill. Humor I could have never rehearsed seeps into my sentences, and then, as well, an intelligence—no—I mean a learnedness as I find myself speaking of eighteenth-century autobiography as the venerable antecedent to the modern memoir, confessional writing rooted in a spiritual, Augustinian tradition, how respect for the form has been lost in its ever-increasing popularity, its brash marketization. This is not a lecture on my book. This is a lecture on the modern memoir, about which, I suddenly find, I am passionate and perceptive, historically rooted, contextualized, academic, scholarly, and a strange thing happens. My body changes. My body is all in my mind. I grow slim and tailored, with a precise mouth and tapered fingers lightly stained with ink. I am no longer wearing a tent for a dress. I am wearing a linen suit, a single gold chain, a dark blue blazer with gold buttons on the cuffs. I feel giddy and enormously happy. This must be hormonal. This must be mania. My pregnant mind has birthed a paradox, has birthed me manly, and I love it.

Later on, dinner with professors and a few graduate students. Platter upon platter of Cambodian food is brought to the table by waiters who whisk away before they become quite visible. The table is long, thirteen, fourteen people; I sit next to the bearded chair of the English Department, and across from me, a bedazzled looking graduate student, handsome in the tattered, smoky way of the burgeoning literary critic, his long hair pulled back in a ponytail. He is impressed by me. I am, after all, the guest of honor. He speaks to me intently, leaning across a mound of white rice. He is young.

Someone pours me tea. I drink it. It does not taste like tea, although it is warm. It tastes like licorice, or alcohol. A few brown flakes float in the unnamed brew, and my contentedness intensifies, my confidence climbs; when the chair of the department tells a fine joke, I laugh and touch him on the arm.

I am much too happy to go to sleep. I realize this after the dinner is over and I'm back at the hotel. The world seems wide with possibility. Therefore, I go into the bar. There is no reason why a woman cannot sit at a hotel bar and sip some soda water, squeeze some lime. The graduate student just happens to be there—I really had no idea—perched on a stool; he pats the seat next to him. I climb aboard.

A bar can be so many things—cheesy, sleazy, elegant, smoky. Tonight it is exotic. Cherries bright as blood cells float in red fluid. Crescent cashews with crystals of salt lie sparkling in glass dishes. He orders a beer. I order a Perrier, and then—I don't know why, I am dizzy, I am drunk on something, the strange Cambodian tea, perhaps, the intoxicant of my own confused confidence, which makes me manly on the one hand but feeling, suddenly, oh so feminine on the other—I add, "with a spritz of white wine please."

I'm thirty-one weeks pregnant, past the point where a little wine could possibly harm the fetus. Our drinks come.

His name, by the way, is Harold, an ugly name for a beautiful boy. What a beautiful boy he is! Close to him now, I can see blond fuzz on his lip, each fingernail clear as abalone. We sip. We speak. We speak. We sip. I will blame it on the wine, which must be mixing with my hormones in the oddest way, for soon my head is floating free from my neck, and I can feel myself *be both*, male and female, brain in the stratosphere, measuring the density of the cumulus clouds with scientific precision, body waterlogged and pleasured in the liquid space below.

We talk for a long time. My head does all the talking. It is graduate student stuff, long-winded and boring, even outdated, Marcuse and Lacan, who in truth I have never understood, but I can do it. I can speak it. It is midnight, and bells go off. It is 1:00 A.M. and the bar is closing. I'm tired now. I'm old. I'm so much older than he.

We walk out into the lobby. "Well," I say. "Shall we go to your room?" he says. I can't believe this. Shall we go to my room? I am married. I am pregnant. He is no more than twenty-six. He is utterly direct. "To your room?" he repeats, and I keep blinking.

"Yes," I say. I don't know why. I blame it on the wine, the Cambodians, the hormones, the double X of my fixed chromosomes, which are tilted toward womanly deceit. In truth, I don't know why. His youth attracts me. I have never been attracted by youth before. I like his idealism. I like that he loves Baudelaire. I like that his life is wide open, that he can smoke clove cigarettes until dawn each day, that no umbilical cord roots him to reality.

All of the above is hogwash, an excuse. The truth is, I just say yes, and the elevator doors luridly part to reveal a pink interior chamber with plush seats and a little toy doorman, ineffectively guarding the entrance. We step in.

On the hotel's fourteenth floor, I unlock my door, and we cross over. Perhaps I should also add here that Jacob and I, of late, have been sleeping in separate beds. We are not fighting. He has attended every birth class with me and has long stopped suggesting silly names. However, he is determined to be up by five and at work by six each morning, and I cannot fall asleep until midnight at least, with my belly so big, with the baby's evening gymnastics pounding.

"Don't turn on the lights," he says when I turn them on. I turn them off. I am getting scared. I am out of control. I am aroused, and enjoying the feeling, which has not happened for months and months, my body coming back to me in this specific way.

"I want to make love to you," he says. I nod, not necessarily in assent, but then he is coming toward me, his hand on the back of my neck, and then he gently, awe-fully places his hand on my stomach.

This is when the spell snaps. He places his hand on my stomach. I leap backward. It is not the breast that is private; it's the belly. When this boy, Harold, touches me *there*, I feel he has touched my marriage, what is between me and Jacob, a place he has no right to tread.

"I'm sorry," I say. "This is absurd," I say. "I can't do this,"

I say. "Why not?" he asks, and I say, "Do you really want to have sex with a married pregnant lady?" and he says, "Yes, I find your body beautiful."

"Thank you," I say. "I am really flattered, but I can't go through with this. I am married to a man I love. I am tired and using poor judgment. You have to go."

And so, just like that, he goes. Perhaps he was never really here. Except this. I can still feel his hand. Even after he's gone, I can still feel his hand on my stomach, a wrongful weight. I shower. In the drumming water I think of Eva, and if she sensed the weight where she was, and if it hurt her.

April 25

Logan Airport. Landing plane. Cab ride home. As soon as I step in the house, I put my arms around Jacob. "We have a mouse problem," he says. "I've been setting traps. This house is infested."

"I miss you," I say. "I want to sleep in the same bed again," I say. "Why do you have to go to sleep so early each night? Why do you have to get to work at the crack of dawn? You're pushing yourself way too hard."

"It's temporary," he says. "It's just until Eva comes. I have to do everything I can do at work now, so I'll be able to take time off to spend with Eva."

I pull back, look at him. His eyes seem faded, a pale, boiled blue, and there is, in general, a sunkenness about his appearance. "Jacob," I say. I press two fingers to his face.

May 1

I have dinner with my friend Jennifer. Every week we meet. At least a few times a week I talk on the phone to Elizabeth, to my sister, to Lisa, to Molly, the smartest couch potato I've ever known. Sitting in a booth across from Jennifer, who is so beautiful and so extraordinarily kind, I realize how much I love my friends, how every one is a sister to me, how, in the absence of family, they are comfort and trust. I want my friends with me always. I want to grow old with them. They are as important to me as Jacob, as Eva, maybe more. They bring me tiny sunbonnets, teething rings, rattles.

May 2

Tonight, I look at the seven other couples in the birth class with us. I do not know their names, despite the fact that, every week, we come together and practice intimate exercises. Not once has the instructor talked about parenting after the baby is born. Instead, we fetishize labor. We focus on it to the exclusion of each other, our children, our futures. Is this because it can be taught, and parenting can't? Because, Americans to the bitter end, we love a sport, grow bored by things more subtle?

Our instructor, Joanne, looks like an athlete. She could not have more than 10 percent body fat. Sometimes, when she leans over so her shirt falls forward, I think I can see the pink haze of her heart beneath the integument she calls skin. Veins, taut and ropy, climb up her arms. The entire class she teaches in a squat position.

"This is our fourth class," Joanne says, "and tonight we're going to talk about anesthesia and painkillers in birth. We're going to look at the data."

Still in her squat, she edges over to the whiteboard, picks up the thick red marker. "Research shows," she says, "that women who have had epidurals do not bond as well with their babies. There's a flatness to the whole experience for them. Research also shows," she says, "that there is a high and compelling correlation"—and here she draws a bold, upward-pointing arrow on the board—"between technologically assisted births and maternal depression afterwards."

She pauses to let this sink in. I eye Jacob. I have always planned on using whatever pain medications are available to me. I hear Joanne say, "Natural childbirth makes every woman a heroine," and then, I cannot help it, I want to be a heroine, I have an image of myself birthing in a Batman mask and a deep red cape; I start to smile and the image changes: here I am, a brave sheen of sweat on my face, eyes inward from the pain that tourniquets my insides, cutting off the blood supply. I can do it. I can do it. Crowds cheer. A ball floats over the cervical rim, comes down, down through the webbed net, we have our hands extended. I can do it. All of us can do it. We watch the instructor raptly, attentively, for we see she is offering us a chance, a woman's only chance, she seems to say, at bravery.

May 4

I am given signs. *This is what to do.* I am at the office the next day, and my client Suzanne brings me basil so fresh our session is scented with it, leafy greens bunched on my desk—*Go natural.* When the session is over and I am alone, I taste the basil, tearing off the tip of a frond, placing pure flavor on my tongue.

But who can really easily read the signs? First, there was basil. Second, there is Ellie. Her last name is Good. She comes in for her session right after Suzanne. She's one of my favorite clients, sixty years old, voice hoarse from so many cigarettes, tummy huge with tumors she will not let the doctors touch. She lowers herself into the seat across from me.

She smiles. She smiles slowly and intentionally, as she does every week, and then she pats her swollen stomach. "My my," she says. "Mama Lauren," she says, "you are getting very *big.*"

"I know," I say. "Some basil?" I say, offering her a taste.

"Can't eat it," she says. "My colitis."

I nod.

"I want to give you some advice," she says.

I try to look neutral but, in fact, I love getting advice

from my patients. Some of the best guidance in my life has come from them. Now Ellie leans forward, leans right over her bulging belly, and says, "Take it from me."

"Okay," I say smiling. "I will."

"I'm going to butt into your life," she says, "just like you've butted into mine. You're a kid," she says. "I could be your grandmother."

"Not quite," I say. "Really, I'm older than I look."

"I know how old you are," she says, and I'm briefly taken aback, for I have never told her. "I have intuitive powers," she says. I shrug. It's possible.

"And my intuition tells me," she says, "that you are actually thinking about giving birth to a baby without drugs."

I eye her warily.

"So let me tell you a little story," she says in her raspy voice. She licks her lips. I smell the cigarette smoke in her clothes, in her coarse red hair. "I had my first baby three weeks early. This was a long, long time ago, before they had all the good stuff, the spinals and stuff. I was in the hospital and all these women were screaming. I started to scream too. I was trying not to, biting down so hard I had holes in my tongue."

She pauses, gives a dramatic flourish with her hand, sticks out her tongue, and points. "You see those little holes?" she says, tongue now tucked back in. "The marks are still there."

All I can do is nod. In fact, I could not see any holes in her tongue, but I don't want to be a sour sport. I realize we are here making myths that are, at the same time, absolutely true.

"So," she continues, "I was biting down so hard I got these holes in my tongue. I was trying not to scream but the pain, the *pressure*, I couldn't help it. I screamed and Dr. Marina came in and said, 'All you women just be quiet. You've had babies before, most of you, so what are you screaming about?'

"And I said to him, 'Dr. Marina, do you know what this pain is like? Do you know what you're talking about? Unless you've had your dick pierced, don't tell me to be quiet.' "

And here, in the story, Ellie breaks into a huge grin. She guffaws and rocks back in her chair. "He was a good man," Ellie continues. "He told me I was right. And then my baby was coming. Back then, they didn't have fancy beds or Jacuzzis. They'd put you on a marble slab—it was freezing—so when you messed yourself it was easy to wipe up. I lay on a marble slab from Monday at five A.M. to Friday at seven P.M. That's how long my labor was. I don't know how I survived. I don't believe in natural childbirth—I pray you don't either—because the drugs, they are important. They are necessary for most women, unless you're like my sister Annette, who has a very wide vagina and just poops her kids out. She pooped one out in the bathtub, one while she was still in her street clothes. But most women, Lauren, most women aren't like that."

She stops, folds her hands Buddha-like over her belly.

She presses her lips together and gives a single firm nod. "Take it from me," she says.

I will.

May 9

Because, if I am going to use drugs, which I think I will, we sign up for a one-day crash course in childbirth at the hospital. It is taught by a nurse who passes out pamphlets picturing the long epidural needle, the woman curled in a fetal position on her side. We learn that we will lose our legs as sensation ceases in the body's lower half, and that this numbness will be a great gift and a loss, "because you cannot really feel your baby coming out," the nurse says. "Still," she says, "most women experience the epidural as an incredible relief from intense pain."

I raise my hand.

"Yes," she says.

"Can you think," I say, "of any compelling reason not to use the epidural in childbirth?"

The nurse pauses. "Actually no," she says. "You don't get your tooth pulled without Novocain. Why would you do this without something similar?"

I sit back in my seat. I look around the room—at the women, not their partners. The faces are inscrutable. "How many of you," asks the instructor, "plan on using the epidural?" You would think, after her sales pitch, that all fifty hands would rocket up, but instead the hands rise slowly, shamefully, eyes cast down at the ground. I am among the ambivalent as my own hand hovers in the sterile air. And yet, at the same time, I'm aware of the contradiction, because every day I swallow drugs. I have been swallowing drugs for years and years, I don't look back, I don't regret, I never think, *I should make it on my own.* I have long ago accepted that my mind cannot make it on its own, that I must, neurologically speaking, cobble through on a crutch. Therefore, perhaps I long for one place to prove my strength, one arena in which I can shine, robust and muscular and absolutely anatomically correct.

The second half of the class the nurse devotes to complications. I learn that the baby's cord can fall into the vagina, that the placenta can rip from the wall of the uterus with the same loud, painful rasp as bark torn from a tree. None of this scares me. In fact, I find it far less jangling than the natural childbirth class, where we are told, over and over again, that birthing should be a simple and primitive release.

I am a child of Western medicine. I am a cynic, a skeptic, which is the attitude underlying so much of Western medicine. I don't believe in inherent goodness. I don't believe that nature will never lead you astray. I believe there are more than one hundred billion cells in the body and if, at any moment, one of them is not becoming cancerous, it's only your good luck, the whimsy of your god that has spared you. Natural childbirth proudly announces, "All pain has a purpose," which is a wonderful view, an utterly Romantic view, straight out of the mind of Shelley or Byron; those thoughts are not mine. I live in a world of random events, unseen collisions, and sudden swerves. The beauty, for me, lies not in knowing there is an underlying purposeful pattern but in facing, with some sort of grace, the impenetrable vista.

And the nurse, as though reading my thoughts, says, "Now we come to the hard part. You should prepare yourselves, emotionally speaking, for the highly unlikely event of a death."

All the ions in the air go still. All eyes go fixed, forward; no one says a word. "It is so highly unlikely," the nurse says. "In all my years at the Brigham we have had only one maternal death. Nevertheless, sometimes there are complications with the baby, with the mother, life-or-death decisions need to be made, how long do you use life support for, to what extent do you want your medical team to artificially prolong a mother's or an infant's existence. It is best," the nurse says, "to talk about these things ahead of time, amongst yourselves. Don't dwell on them, please, but the husbands should be ready to assume decision making of the most difficult kind. That's it," she says. "That's all we need to say about this highly unlikely event."

When we leave the class, the sun is setting. It looks loose and enormous. Blackbirds fly in front of it, dotting the sickest of stars with dark moles, melanomas. I squint up. Jacob takes my hand. We say not a word.

By the time we get home, the air is darkening rapidly.

Our dogs sit in the window, watching us approach the front door. Musashi, the male, lifts his paw and scratches at the glass. Inside, he wreathes around our ankles, whimpers and nudges with his nose. "What's wrong, Musashi? Musashi, what's wrong?" I say.

I flip on the hall light. I tread toward the kitchen. I flip on the kitchen light. I see a mouse streak across the counter, disappear into a hole in our blue wall. I see another mouse scurry beneath the fridge. "Oh my God," I say. I go over to the sink for a glass of water, and just as I turn on the tap I see a gray shape right next to the disposal; I scream, look down, and there, hunched in the basin, are two brown baby mice. "What is it?" Jacob says, running in.

"There are mice in the sink," I say. We edge toward the counter again, peer over. The mice are scared, frantic, trying to climb the chrome walls, falling back flat on their little backs; it disgusts me, it saddens me. Jacob was right; we are infested.

Jacob takes another step forward. The mice lunge at the chrome cliffs in one last desperate attempt and then, unable to scale the heights, fall back, fall this time, to our horror, straight down the open disposal.

Jacob and I stand still, staring at each other. His face looks unnaturally white. We can hear the rodents' panicked chirping amidst the gears and vegetable waste. "We have no choice," Jacob says. "We have to grind them up."

"You can't grind them up," I say. "We can't do that." I hear my voice tight, high, edging on hysteria. "That's a terrible way to die. We have to fish them out, set them free."

We lean over the disposal, peer down. We cannot see them. We can only hear them.

"There is no way," Jacob says, "to fish them out."

"Well then," I say, my tongue dry, "we'll drown them. We're not going to grind them up. We can't!"

"We can't drown them," Jacob says, his eyes huge and startled. "That's even crueler. It's a slow death."

We stand there looking at each other, staring, really, frozen on the kitchen floor. The image of the nurse floats through my mind, the long needle of the epidural, the cracked placenta, the sick sun. In the highly unlikely event.

"We need to make a decision," I say, "that's right for both of us. I do not want the live mice ground up."

"I do not," he says, "want to drown two baby animals. My stepfather used to do that and it's cruel, I'm telling you it's the cruelest way to die."

"Well then, maybe we should throw some poison down there. Maybe that's the way to do it."

"Okay," he says, "like what?"

I fling open cupboards looking for some tasty poison, some kind way to kill. All I find, of course, are cereals, sugars, bagels, bread. I have the brief, absurd idea that I should call an ambulance, the Animal Rescue League. "There's nothing here," I say.

"Just let me handle this," Jacob says. The nurse says, *The husbands should be ready to assume.* "It will be over in a minute."

I walk into the living room. I have been aware, all

through this pregnancy, of how much can go wrong. The brain can go so terribly wrong, the future feels fierce, the past threatens to transmogrify, questions carry you in rickety baskets borne by pocked balloons; everything bumps. You hang on. You try to have some grace.

I hear Jacob opening the cabinet door, where the switch to the disposal sits. Who can avoid imagining it, the fur and shards, the wordless fear? I put my head in my hands, and then my hands over my ears as the machine starts, picks up speed, and the animals disappear in a swirl of flesh, melted into molecules, dropping down the drain and into the pipes of the house where I live with a man, two dogs, a baby, a yard, squirrels and worms and other prowling things.

LABOR

―――――

June 8

We are having a heat wave. Inefficient breezes paddle at the swollen air. I drink gallons of lemonade, snap cool sheets over the bed.

Jacob kisses me good night. In my separate bed, I read late. Tonight, the baby barely kicks.

Sometime later I wake to a sharp pang, very intense, but oh so brief, like a scalpel whisked across the stomach.

Five-thirty A.M. Was that a labor pain? I climb out of bed; I have no idea why. And that is when I hear it. I hear it first, before I feel it, a little pop, like an internal cork from a private champagne bottle; I bubble over. My waters break.

Where is Jacob? What should I do? The water keeps pouring. "Catch it," the doctors had said. "Catch it in a cup and make sure it's clear." Clear water is good, but water with even a tinge of green means something called meconium, signaling, possibly, a fetus in distress.

I run around my room, leaking and looking for a cup;

no cup; I cup my hands, catch my own cool flow. Is it clear? Is it green? I bring my cupped palms close to my face, peer into the pool there, but before I can tell its color, the water leaks away.

I'm panicked but also enjoying myself. Having your waters break, especially in the middle of a heat wave, is lovely. You are so turgid, so waddling, so sloshy, and then at long last the amniotic cloud rips its lining and rains out all that weight.

I thought when one's waters broke that there would be a pint, at most a quart. But it keeps coming. And I keep stupidly running around my room, looking for a cup, spattering the floor as I go. And then, just as suddenly, the flow stops. There is a sharp, quick cramp. I sit on the bed.

On my white sheet I see a water stain that is, indeed, green. Not very green, but definitely not clear. Meconium is considered an emergency because if the baby breathes it in she could burn her lungs. "Jacob," I shout.

No answer.

"Ja-cob!" I shout again.

"What is it?" he says, coming in stumbling and bed-headed.

"I'm in labor," I say. I say it with a flourish. I say it with drama and self-satisfaction. I say it, and I know, as I do, that those three words—*I'm in labor*—will elicit a response from him stronger than any sexy tidbit I might mutter in his ear, than any adultery I might someday admit. What power.

Sure enough, his sleepy eyes go wide, just like a cartoon dad's. "Now?" he asks.

"My waters broke," I say. "But listen, we have to call the doctor. There's meconium in the fluid."

Jacob scratches his head, settles back into himself. The mention of meconium does not alarm him; it calms him, like any scientific or medical phenomenon.

"Meconium," he says. "How do you know that?"

"Look," I say, pointing to the sheet. "That's where my waters first broke. And the stain is green."

Jacob walks over to the sheet, bends to study it like it's some sort of text. After a long, thoughtful pause he pronounces, "The stain is not green."

"What do you mean it's not green?" I say. "It's obviously green, and they told us if it was green to call the doctor right away because it could be a medical emergency. . . ."

I hear my words get fast, jumbled. I often do this in response to Jacob's analytical calmness. The more thoughtful and ponderous he becomes, the more I insist on making him see the situation as a crisis.

"Look again, Lauren," he says. "That's not green."

I peer again at the sheet. "It's green," I retort.

"No," he says. "You're being pessimistic. There's a faint tinge to it, but that's coming from the light reflecting through the window. Your water's clear."

"It's green!" I scream.

A pain has twisted up my uterus. It's actually not a bad pain, a very brief pain, but I decide to make the most of it anyway. "I'm in pain!" I shout.

Jacob looks at me. I look at him. Just at that moment another flood of water sluices between my thighs, my God, a gallon gone by now; how much more could there be?

It gushes onto the floor, surfing over Jacob's bare toes; the sheer volume, the sheer force, I don't know. He backs away.

I pick up the phone, have the OB paged. Jacob and I wait in silence for her return call. I start to feel odd, not physically but mentally, a dampness, a depression. I'm in labor, my whole life tilting toward the unknown, and outside the sky is gray. Good-bye good-bye. I've made enough water for a small ocean, on which my ship is sailing. Already, my beloved blue dresser on the opposite wall looks tiny in the distance, the wall itself as hazy as any horizon. The phone chirps. I pick it up.

"This is Dr. Green," the OB says.

You've got to be kidding, I think.

"This is Lauren Slater," I say. "I'm thirty-six weeks pregnant and my waters just broke and"—I look at Jacob—"and there might be a very faint tinge of green in the fluid." I pause. "We're not sure," I say.

"Pack your bags," Dr. Green says. "And get to the hospital. Immediately."

We drive off in the dawn. I cry when I kiss the dogs good-bye. I feel so bad for the dogs. They have no idea what misery awaits them. They are such quiet, dignified dogs, they will never understand a baby's screaming. I lift Musashi's sweet, wet muzzle to my mouth and say, "Don't worry, you'll always be my firstborn."

I lift Lila's pointy, sweet muzzle to my mouth and say,

"You'll always be my second born, and my first girl." Lila, in response, licks my lips, and I'm so moved by this I lick her lips back.

"The dogs are not your children," Jacob says to me now. He says this every time I speak of them as human kin, which is often. "Eva is your child," Jacob announces. "The dogs," he says, "are your roommates."

And then we are off. I look back at the house and think that never again will it be my house in just the same way. I look at my neighborhood as we careen down the streets; the next time I walk these streets, it will be as a different woman, a *mother, mother, mother.* "The dogs are not my roommates," I burst out to Jacob in the car. "As far as I'm concerned those dogs are my children, I'm going to love them just as much as Eva, so don't expect me to pay any less attention to them once the baby comes, I would never, *never* relegate my dogs to second status, it's just plain human hubris that you would, for all we know dogs are better than people, I like them better anyway because I don't even like people that much, which I told you, didn't I tell you that, why are we having this baby?" I stop. Abruptly. Jacob brakes for a red light. The car gets very quiet and then I whisper, "Listen. Jacob. Are you sure you want this baby?"

He starts to laugh. "It's a little late now," he says.

"Listen," I say. "I hope you really want this baby, because I just decided I don't."

"I want the baby," he says. "Even if you don't, I do." He puts his hand on my knee.

"I need to know," I say, "that you will take total, one hundred percent responsibility for it because I'm not going to love it. I'm incapable of love. I'm mentally unsound."

"One hundred percent," he says.

I know he's humoring me, but it helps, it really does.

"The poor baby," I say. "I hate to think of her breathing in meconium."

"I thought you were incapable of caring," he says.

We ride for a little longer in silence. He rests one hand on the back of my neck, and the touch, his touch, means so much to me. A cramp comes, this one significant, my uterus balling up and flaming. "Is that a contraction?" Jacob says.

"Yeah," I say. I breathe through it.

"Shit," he says, which I think is so funny, given the meconium situation, that I start to laugh and then cry. "We're in a fucking traffic jam," Jacob says.

The contraction subsides. Ahead of us, the drawbridge is up and an obese boat is huffing its way oh so slowly to the other side. "This is going to take a fucking hour," Jacob says. I contract again. Jacob whips out his stopwatch to time it. "Breathe breathe breathe," he says, his role to relax me while, meanwhile, caught in a clutch of cars in a Boston rush hour, the cords in his neck look alive with tension. "Breathe breathe breathe," he says and presses on his horn with the heel of his hand.

I feel the contraction peak and then leave, very gently it leaves, like a breeze.

And just as it subsides, more water comes, the most so far. I am pure spigot, only this time the fluid feels different, thicker and hotter. "I have to check my pad," I say.

I don't care that there are cars in lanes on either side of us, nor do I care about dignity, that concept I've been grumbling about all through my pregnancy. I heave myself up off the seat and whisk down my shorts while onlookers stare—what do I care? The pad is soaked with pea soup, a dark, swampy green, and the baby breathes it all in, burning.

The good news is we get to the hospital before I pop the infant out. Soaking, and smelling like a bog in an industrial town, I arrive in obstetrical triage, where the doctor on call, Dr. Epstein, snaps on latex gloves and checks me for dilation. "Well," she says, withdrawing her hand. "You're only one, maybe two centimeters, but there's no doubt about the meconium. We're going to induce. Do you have a problem with that?" she asks. She doesn't wait for my answer, or for Jacob's. Jacob and I stare at each other across the examination room. I shrug. He shrugs back, the first time I've ever seen him admit to not knowing, to insecurity. "Okay," Dr. Epstein says to the nurse, "get this lady a room, get her an IV, get her on antibiotics, let's Pit her now."

"Pit her?" Jacob says. His voice here sounds so small, so unsure.

"Pit," Dr. Epstein says, "short for Pitocin, a chemical we use to force labor on."

"Why," says Jacob, "do you have to force her labor? She's already started. Does she need that drug, that Pitocin?"

Dr. Epstein turns to him slowly. "Are you questioning my judgment?" she says.

Jacob, to my delight, says, "Yes."

"Yes?" Dr. Epstein echoes.

"Yes, I am questioning your judgment, but," Jacob adds, all diplomacy and grace, "solely out of my own ignorance. Could you explain why doctors induce when a labor is already on its way?"

"Time," Dr. Epstein says. "Because in this case, we are short on time."

I am wheeled into a labor and delivery room. I get a green gown with tiny snowflakes on it. Dr. Epstein, to my dismay, is a Laura Ashley gal; she is dressed in a cinched flowery skirt, a crisp white top that would turn even the merest fleck of blood into a beacon. Around her, I am embarrassed of my body. I feel like I'm in my high school Latin class, surrounded by a strange language I should have studied last night but didn't. I don't know my declensions. I will be called upon. I don't know my *hic haec hocs*. She will call upon me. I will have nothing but silence to summon as my answer. She will fail me. This, the doctor who will deliver me.

A blond, blue-eyed nurse comes into the room. "I'm Ingrid," she says. She pushes up my hospital johnny and attaches several suckers to my belly. "Fetal monitor," Epstein explains. Immediately the room reverberates with the sound of Eva's clicking heart. Ingrid slides an IV into my hand. "Is that the Pitocin?" I ask. My voice shakes. I am scared of Dr. Laura Ashley, scared of Nurse Ingrid, who I am suddenly, irrationally sure is an anti-Semite, but most of all I'm scared of the Pitocin. I know all about it. A powerful hormone, it hurls your body into hard, fast labor—there is no slow building for the Pitted patient; once the drug hits, you are wrenched in cramps.

"Here's the Pitocin," Epstein says, handing a bag to Ingrid, who attaches it to the IV. I want to say, "No. Stop." I'm not at all convinced we need to induce this quickly. After all, the baby's heartbeat and vital signs are fine. Part of me wonders if this induction is for the doctor's convenience—get it over by lunch—or is this the medical establishment's typical aggressive approach? But then again, there is meconium. Is meconium truly serious? We feel we know nothing. In fact we know nothing! How silent Jacob and I have become here at the birth of our baby, who will learn, from us, how to talk.

It is not possible that I hear the Pitocin entering my veins, but I do, a sound like water dripping down a drain—kerplink, kerplink—and I wait on the bed for its effects while Jacob, ashen-looking, sits across from me in a special reclining chair "just for dads." He seems fuzzy, out of focus. The clock on the wall is a huge schoolroom clock, the black hands twitching time forward, sideways, backward, where are we? Eleven A.M. We have been in this room for four hours already, but I thought only a moment had passed. Kerplink. Kerplink. Down the hall a woman screams. I mean that absolutely. Her scream has the sound of murder in it, a bad slasher movie, an infant's jumpy cry, and then gone. Silence. I strain to see my husband; in that chair for dads he looks so distant. "Can you come here?" I say. I want to touch him before the pain is upon me, before the pain seals me into a selfish world where only I exist.

He comes to me, holds my hands. "So this is it," he says. "In a couple of hours we'll be parents."

"Yeah," I say. I reach down, beneath my gown, touch the creamy globe that is my belly. Touch the hardened knob of my navel. Feel the slopes and peaks, the running rivers of veins that increased blood flow has brought to the surface of my skin; soon, like a soufflé, it will all collapse, the pregnancy gone, thank God, and yet I think I will actually miss it a little, this time of pure potential.

"Put your hand on my belly," I say to Jacob.

He does.

"This is huge," he says.

I must fall asleep because suddenly, before I can prepare, the contractions are upon me and I'm rearing my head off the pillow. Nurse Ingrid is in the room—when did she enter?—her long fingers turning the dial on the Pitocin monitor. "Just upping your dosage," she tells me, smiling, her perfect side teeth curved like cashews, an obscene speck of scarlet lipstick sparkling on a fang. And then she disappears. Just like that. Just like a *Star Trek* character, she does not leave so much as melt from sight, and in her place a pain I am not prepared for. The sensation is sound and motion both, keening into a crescendo and then shattering down; there is glass on the floor. A vase has been broken. "It's started," I say to Jacob. "This is it. Hard labor."

My friend Elizabeth, to whom I have promised a front-row seat, rushes into the room; I must have called her, or Jacob must have. At some point my sister Tracy will arrive. "She's just begun," Jacob says to her.

"You wouldn't believe the traffic," Elizabeth says.

"Didn't you just get a new car?" Jacob says.

"A Subaru," Elizabeth says.

Another contraction comes upon me, but apparently they can't tell. They continue their conversation about Subarus and air bags and the general condition of the automotive industry as I feel the twist and heat. "Shut up!" I scream at them, and I try to focus on staying afloat— *breathe and relax, breathe and relax*—and then the pain passes.

"Okay," I say to them. "You can't talk while I'm having contractions. It distracts me."

I try extra hard to make my voice reasonable, polite, because what I really want to do is snarl and claw, some primitive impulse, I feel my lip curl back. I am an animal. I seek the cool of a private cave, a dirt den, a grove where every leaf is green. Shhh.

And shatter, again. And again. My uterus balls up, tries to buck the baby out. J and E sit silent, stare. They no longer have names to me. They barely exist for me, yet if they were to leave me, I would panic.

Five minutes pass, ten minutes pass, I look up at the clock on the wall but, no, it is dusk already, ten hours have passed. How long have I been at this? Outside the hospital window a plane moves menacingly through the air; it is shining like a syringe in the late-day summer light, squirting fuel into the skin of the sky, and when the next contraction comes I close my eyes against such a sight, the intense and irritating stimulation of the visual, and I try to fly with the cramps. I do every breathing pattern I've been taught, but the pain is bigger than I, it must come out, and that is when it happens. I start to sing.

I never knew such songs existed in me. I never knew, until labor, the power of sound to contain and expel pain. I am not talking about nursery rhymes or folk tunes; I am talking the song of the cow, the bellow of the bull as a kosher knife shears off the tender testicles. I am talking the cat song at midnight, when mating season is here and the rhododendrons are in profuse, excessive bloom. When the next contraction comes I open my mouth— what a gift from God, our mouths, those magnificent exit doors, the red lips all lit up like emergency signs in a movie theater, what a gift. When the next contraction comes I open my mouth and low, drawing the sound up from the deepest part of my stomach, and it helps. I am carried off to a hill in Vermont where once, when I was twelve years old, I slept against the warm flank of a cow, bees buzzing in the summer field. There was, then, the smell of cut grass and spools of hay, all golden in the heat.

This goes on for I don't know how long. I low my way through labor. At one point I get up and empty my bowels into the toilet, that should take care of the shitting on the table concern. Nurses come in and out of the room, changing bloody pads. "How far along am I?" I ask. They won't say. Since my waters have broken they want to keep internal exams to a minimum, because there is now a higher risk of infection.

Darkness comes. My vocal cords are raspy. "I want to know how far along I am," I say, I whine. Ingrid comes in and ratchets up the dial. She smiles in a wicked way. The next contraction, then, is beyond cow, beyond bull, beyond any bellow I could ever make, and when it's over I say, "All right. Painkillers."

E runs out of the room to get the doctor. In moments Epstein is beside my bed, only she looks different. She looks kinder. In the soft evening light of the room I see her hair has some gray in it, and when she rests her hand on my leg the gesture seems so gentle to me I want her just to take me to her house and feed me toast and tea. "Are you ready for the epidural?" she murmurs. "Yes," I say. I am so small. She is so strong. I am so helpless, she the source of all help. She parts my legs. "You're four centimeters dilated," she says. "That's far enough along. We'll go get you some relief."

If you have ever sat outside, on a porch, during a summer storm and watched the rain fall fast and thick, and heard the thunder in every cloud, and then seen, over time, a slant of sun peek through—if you have ever witnessed such a sight and felt, within your body, the distinct sensation of the passing of a summer storm, the humid air becoming thrillingly clear, then you know just what an epidural feels like.

It is quite amazing. After the needle, I lie very still and listen to the storm travel off until at last the whole swirl of weather has moved miles and miles away, where I can hear it still, feel the contractions still, but without threat or intensity.

Two-thirty A.M. Almost twenty-four hours since my waters have broken. Jacob and Elizabeth look exhausted. I, on the other hand, feel elated. "This is so awesome," I say. "Why would anyone ever even *consider* giving birth without an epi?"

"Epi?" Jacob says.

I pick up the phone, call my sister Tracy, despite the fact that it's 2:00 A.M. Oh well, she was always a night owl. "Hey, Trace," I say. "Guess where I am?" I had promised her she, too, could be at the birth.

"Epi?" Jacob keeps saying. He and Elizabeth eye each other. Then Jacob comes over to read the ingredients listed on the IV bag that contains this very special anesthetic.

"Tell me there's morphine in it," I sing. "There's no way this is just local Novocain. There's heroin in this. I feel too good."

Sure enough, there is some morphine derivative added to the epidural, making it a mighty cocktail indeed.

"Bless them," I say.

Dr. Epstein pokes her head into the room. "Better use this time to get some sleep," she says. "You'll be ready to push this baby out before you know it."

"Good idea," Jacob says, opening his recliner. "I'm exhausted."

"Sleep?" I say, after Dr. Epstein leaves. "Are you kidding me? I don't want to sleep. I want to celebrate."

And so we do. After all, I am queen for the day. I get whatever I want. It is 2:30 A.M. and we watch TV. I pay absolutely no attention to what's on the screen. I just keep gushing about the wonders of the epidural. I want to connect. Only connect, Forster says. He was such a smart man, such a brilliant artist, and so am I. I have so much talent, so much potential, it's insane I haven't really been confident of this before; really, I should write an epic novel, something broad and historical and also political, something with some political punch; in fact, give me some paper, I'll start right now.

"Settle down, Lauren," Jacob says.

"I'm down I'm down," I sing, which is literally true. With the epidural flowing through a needle taped into my spine, I am no longer allowed to move, to eat, to drink, to pee, to shit. Nurse Ingrid inserts a catheter, and my urine flows out, all honey.

How pretty I am.

June 10

"Just cut the baby out now," Jacob demands.

"She's seven centimeters dilated," Dr. Epstein says. "She's slow, but making progress. The baby's vital signs are fine. On the monitor the baby looks great. We'd like to avoid a C-section if at all possible."

"It's been forty-five hours," Jacob says.

"Forty-five hours," I echo. My lips feel huge and cracked, the thirst intolerable. True, I'm numb from my navel down, but the bliss is gone and in its place I dream of liquids, ginger ale fizzing in my happy face, the wet crackle of a seltzer as you twist the top off and fresh foam spigots out.

"I want some water," I croak. "I need some water."

"No water," Dr. Epstein says. She practically wags her finger at me. "No food or water once you've had the epidural. That is nonnegotiable."

She leaves. I feel I am being punished for surrendering to pain relief. Immediately after the doctor disappears I ring the buzzer for the nurse. Ingrid, thank God, has gone home, and in her place is Ivy, a lovely although somewhat dim-witted twenty-year-old.

"Yes?" Ivy says, appearing in my doorway.

"I'd like some water," I say. "Dr. Epstein approved."

Turns out I'm the one who's dim-witted. Ivy lowers her chin and looks at me. "That's an obvious lie," she says. "It is absolutely against protocol to give a patient liquids when an epidural has been administered. It could kill you."

How, I want to know, could water kill me? Water is the source of all life, the essential lubricant, the single sustaining current.

Ivy explains. What she says makes no sense to me, or to Jacob, for that matter. This whole birth makes no sense to me, or to Jacob, despite how well we thought we prepared, how many classes we took, how many books we read. At the point the Pitocin entered my veins— kerplink, kerplink—we gave up the rudder to a captain we knew nothing of. This was a mistake, but we don't know how we could have done it differently.

Ivy leaves. When she returns she is carrying a cup with a single ice chip, which she spoons into my parched mouth; I feel it melt, glorious and silver. I slip back into sleep.

When I wake again I am not in the same place. Jacob and Elizabeth are gone. I hear an ominous beeping from the IV machine. It is deep in the night, the second night of labor, and through the numbness of the epidural I sense a tremendous pressure in my rectum. It recedes, returns, recedes, returns. *The baby*, I think, *is almost here.*

That beeping though. What is it? I have heard such a

sound before, on TV hospital shows when the cardiac line goes flat. Beep beep beep. You're dead. Am I dying? Is the baby dying? The pressure in my rectum—tremendous. Slowly, I reach my hand down between my legs. I must be dreaming. Where are J and E? I must be dreaming. I feel the baby's fist dangling out of my vagina, I feel all five fingers uncurl, the ragged edges of the tiny nails, she shakes my hand. Hello.

I wake up, this time for real. By my bedside, the phone rings and rings. Who would be calling me here, now, at such an hour? "Hello," I whisper into the receiver.

"Lauren," a voice whispers back at me. I would know that voice anywhere, would know it if it called me from the moon, from beyond the grave—my mother.

I start to cry. "Mom," I say. "Mom. How did you know?"

"Your sister called me," she says. "How is it going?"

"The baby won't come out," I say.

"Well," my mother whispers, "she's a stubborn little girl, just like you."

Somewhere, a machine beeps. A fist pounds, furious. I am bleeding from the butt, giving birth through the butt, the epidural has worn off, too much time gone by, and the smell is pungent, ominous; "Infection," Epstein says.

Thirst, I think.

"C-section," she says. "Failure to progress. Infection starting. Now."

All the lights in my room go on, show's over. Anesthesiologists swarm around my bed, Ivy holds my hand with a pitying look in her eyes—am I going to die? A pale young doctor, the resident anesthesiologist, pricks me with pins. "Can you feel this prick?" he says, and then his face flushes furiously.

A superior numbness now moves from the very tips of my toes, up past my navel, and into my nipples. I am buried beneath an avalanche, stuffed with snow. "Can you feel it here?" the resident says, as he moves his pins and pricks around and, no, I cannot feel it, no I cannot feel it, and a fury rises up in me, pricks and pins and pitted girls, Pitocin, pretty girls, just a little drip of water please, drip drop, kerplink, you could go crazy here, so many hours, these pricks in me, and then I feel it.

To the left of my uterus, just a few inches, there seems to be a spot resistant to the anesthetic. "Can you feel it here?" he asks, and I pause and then say, "No, I can't," even though I can. To the left of my uterus is one small spot, a hot spot, still a little bit alive. Let it hurt. Let it rip. I grit my teeth. Gone crazy.

"Good-bye, Elizabeth," I say as they wheel me into the OR. I wave good-bye to my sister Tracy, too, who has joined us at this spectacle. And then a screen goes up in front of my face. Jacob comes in through swinging doors, dressed in scrubs. "Okay," Epstein says, and they start carving away, and at some point soon after, my daughter is supposedly lifted from me, I don't know when, I don't know if, I cannot even surely say she came from me, for I have witnessed not a thing. I have felt not a thing—except this. The distant whisking of the surgeon's scalpel, the one live spot on my skin, and now the wound, still oozing on my shaved pudendum. Later on, back in the recovery room, too drugged to hold Eva, too drugged to see Eva, I float alone, lightly finger the incision, my new birthmark, the only piece of proof I have.

THE FOURTH TRIMESTER

Motherhood

June 11

I am up. Everyone has gone home. It is a different day. I know this by the weather and light outside my window, sky Crayola blue, sun a simple yellow spot, and by my bedside a mysterious vase of congratulatory tulips; I don't like them. They are ferociously bright, shaped like snake heads.

I am up. I don't mean standing up, for I have no feet that I can feel, no legs that I can feel; I throw back the covers, to check. Sure enough, my legs are still there, but numb from anesthesia. My stomach has been gutted. I touch it, like pressing on pudding. This is my proof. The baby is gone from me. The baby has been born. It is 8:00 A.M. on a Friday, and I am, most definitely, a mother.

So where is the baby? The only things here are these monstrous tulips and a plate of pancakes, which I eat. I drink the little tub of orange juice too, peeling back the tinfoil top and gulping the bright stuff down, so good. What is my baby eating? Who is feeding her? I wonder these things, but not for long. I am just so glad to be done with labor. I am just so happy with the orange juice, with the little pieces of pulp, with the butter melting now, pooling on the pancakes; it's been days without sustenance, and I am starved. I feed myself first.

Then I ring the buzzer. "Could I see my baby?" I say to the nurse who appears. "Of course," she says, and she hurries away. My heart starts to rattle around. I am going to meet her now; where is Jacob? I am going to meet her now, after nine months of angst, imagination, nausea, thumping, fear, anticipation, tracing the outlines against my taut skin, guessing, guessing, it's a foot, no a rump, we'll call her Eva, she's been so close to me for so long, right under my nose, tucked and tight, but I have never, ever met her, and this is the moment, is it not, the moment when you become at last what you have so much feared, crossing the line, the great divide—a mother.

They bring her to me. She has on a little hat, knotted at the top, gnomelike. She is swaddled in several vintage looking cloth blankets, which I love, and which would make for some very snazzy hand towels in my vintage bathroom back at home.

The nurse has a smile on her face as she leans down and places the bundle in my arms. I notice her smile, the tiny generic infant, but mostly, unfortunately, I notice the vintagy looking receiving blankets. "Can I have these blankets when I go home?" I ask.

The nurse looks disturbed. "This is your baby," she says. "We're sorry you didn't get to spend much time with her after your C-section. There were a few complications, you had a bad reaction to the anesthetic, so we had to load you up on morphine."

"Hi, Eva," I say. I force myself to look at her face. The eyes are closed, the tiny lids clamped against me, the hands, so small, clutching at the rim of the blue-striped blanket. I run my thumb along the blue stripe. It is pure cotton, the exact periwinkle of my shower curtain. I want it.

Focus on the baby, I say to myself, but I can't, because her face is so sealed. She's pretty, she has good lips, those little bow-shaped lips, and ears just like seashells, white on the outside, whorled on the inside. But my attention drifts. All I can think of is how to get my hands on a stack of these cotton blankets, with which I could curtain my entire house.

"Are we allowed to take the receiving blankets home with us?" I ask the nurse again. She frowns, shrugs. "Not really," she says. "Is this your first?"

"First and last," I say.

"It takes some time," she says.

Jacob comes. If I had any doubts about his commitment to this project, they are just about dispelled right now. He is all in the flush of new fatherhood. He bounds into the room red-cheeked and ecstatic. "Can you believe this?" he keeps saying. He leans over and looks at Eva. "Oh, little Eva bell," my husband sings. "Oh my God are you gorgeous."

I look up at Jacob. I have just been through days of

labor, and I expect something from him, maybe a bottle of Perrier pulled from a back pocket. I am waterlogged and oozing, my incision burns, my hormones peak and plummet, and bits of afterbirth trickle through the padding, stain the sheets.

"Look at her," he says.

"I see her," I say.

"But even when you see her, you can't get enough of her," Jacob says. "She's a feast for the eyes."

"That's a cliché," I say. "I think I need an ice pack."

Jacob rings the bell for the nurse and says, when she reappears in the doorway, "We need an ice pack," and that's that.

"I don't think she's that pretty," I try again. "All newborns look alike to me."

"Are you kidding me?" Jacob says. "I'd know her anywhere."

"I bet you ten bucks," I say, I snap, "we put her in the nursery with all the other babies, and you wouldn't be able to pick her out."

"Oh, little Eva," Jacob sings, "your mama's in a mood, do you want some food, let's not collude—"

And then, before I can stop him, he plucks her from my arms and waltzes her around the room, while I watch, from the fringe.

I am relieved when he leaves. Secretly, I think Eva might be too. It is night now. If I had to measure my maternal feelings on a scale from one to ten, I'd say zero. I'm not even on the scale. But maybe now, now that he's gone. And the nurse is gone. We are alone at last, my daughter and I. I cup her in the crook of my elbow. She is such a quiet baby. She is so sleepy. Her perpetual look of utter peace unnerves me. Too much Prozac, maybe. The drug has turned her into an angel, and I don't know how to hold an angel. I know, only, how to hold a human.

Carefully, oh so carefully, oh so gingerly, I hold her out at arm's length. "Eva Eva Eva," I call. I say her name out loud for the first time, and as I do I hear how pretty it is, how pealing, like a little bell hung outside a country door. "Eva," I sing, and then I give her the gentlest jiggle, and it works. She opens her eyes for the first time that day, and I see inside her eyes—a shocking blue—and she opens her mouth, so I see inside her mouth—a dripping pink—and then she lets out a cry. The sound warbles up, desperate and raspy—such a cry can make you shudder. Such a cry is ancient, an alarm against predators, a reminder of lurking beasts and other Pleistocene dangers, when we lived in caves. We go so far back. And her cry keeps coming, so I do what any decent human would do, I bring her to me. I try to comfort. "Eva Eva Eva," I sing, a little bell, and she goes back to sleep, but I don't. It is late now. But I keep hearing her cry, that strange primitive sound, so full of barb and need, fang and fear, and all that night I stay awake, shaken.

June 12

I like the hospital. It is full of fresh linen, individually wrapped soaps, Shasta daisies, and drugs. It is the closest to a spa I will probably ever come. The nurses whisk in with my little scrubbed bundle. "Here you are," they say. Today they have put a bow on the baby's cap, a frilly purple affair so the baby looks like a birthday present, and I laugh. None of this is serious. I can give the gift back.

"Don't be so nervous," the nurses say when they see me handle Eva. "She's not going to break, you know."

They laugh at how I hold her. "Oh, she's not as fragile as she seems," the nurses say. They grab Eva by her underarms, lift her up, swing her three times in the air. They pat her roughly with the heels of their palms, swaddle her in blankets in one deft motion as crisply as easing a sliced rye into a waxed paper bag.

Nurse Debbie comes in and helps me out of bed. I can still barely walk, from the surgery. My feet are grossly swollen, a common aftereffect of giving birth. "Your body's water balance is shifting around," she says.

I lean on her arm. She helps me hobble down the hall, and the help seems so enormous to me I want to cry. We pass a plate-glass window that shows the city out there, a city I have lived in my entire life, but it seems to me to be a different city, or is it that I am a different person? The light hits the brick buildings in gold, dramatic sheets; the people hurry to and fro, and they all appear to have baguettes tucked under their arms. I tap on the glass. "Are you all right?" Nurse Debbie says to me.

Forty-eight hours ago I expelled the placenta. Once a woman loses the placenta not only the water balance but the hormone balance in her body shifts dramatically, and thus postpartum depressions sometimes occur. "What is a placenta?" I once asked my OB, and she had a hard time explaining it to me. Is it tissue, fiber, cluster of cells, membranous pouch? Is it oxygen, hemoglobin, lifeline, pillow? Humans expel the placenta and then burn it. Bury it. A massive, blood-rich organ, a vascular inner tube, without it will I sink?

Debbie helps me back into bed. Soon the pediatrician will come and we will have a talk.

"Your baby is beautiful," Dr. Gordon says. She is doing the newborn examination in my room, where I can watch. Jacob is with me. Eva is naked in the bassinet, and a huge surgical sun shines down on her. Truth be told, I have not dared examine my daughter closely yet. I have not yet done the new mother thing, counting the fingers and toes, looking deep in the ear, testing the tautness of the gums. I am afraid. Jacob is afraid. All those drugs during pregnancy.

But now the doctor is here, and the examination is under way, and the light is so bright we cannot help but see. We are forced to see. Her skin looks good, the umbilicus appropriately ugly. She has tremendously long lashes, and a lot of dark hair. I gather my courage, heave my swollen body up to better my view. The doctor is smiling. "So healthy," she keeps saying, and I cannot help but hear relief in her voice. "What toes, what knees," she says, and when little Eva pees in a perfect robust arc, hitting the pediatrician smack in the forehead, the doctor gets only more delighted still, laughing and dripping. "What a bandit," she says.

The doctor listens to the breathing, the chest. She checks for reflexes. She spends a long time. Then she is through.

"She's really gorgeous," the pediatrician says.

"So can we assume the drugs didn't hurt her?" I say. As soon as I've said it, I know I shouldn't have. The pediatrician purses her lips. "Everything checks out," she says, "for now."

Jacob leaves. He kisses me good-bye. I think of what the doctor said, the shape of our baby's future, always curved, a question mark. I lift her from the bassinet as best I can with the incision. Then I do what most mothers do moments after birth. Three days have passed. I count ten fingers. Ten toes. I trace the outline of her spine, press my lips to a soft spot and feel the brain beat.

June 13

I am going home today. I'm up on my waterlogged feet, stuffing everything I can into my black bag. I take the receiving blankets, of course, all eight of them folded in the corner, but I don't stop at that. I take the hospital's disposable bottles, the prepackaged nipples, the cans of formula, the talcum. I empty out the bathroom cupboards—soaps galore, terry-cloth towels, a frenzy comes over me. I take the pillowcase, the sheets, the extra hospital johnnies; I go so far as to try to squeeze the bassinet's mattress into my bag, and it works. By the time I am done, my bag is suspiciously swollen with loot—I must take the hospital home with me, this is what I must do—and my room looks ransacked, emptied. I am ready.

A nurse, holding Eva, accompanies us. She eyes my bag, frowns. She frowns again when she sees our car, Jacob behind the wheel of the four-hundred-dollar station wagon we bought for our new family, four doors, to be sure, each one rusted and banged. This is a car with its own soft spots, corroded holes, an excellent engine.

And then we are off, Eva strapped in. The day is abusively hot. The car has no air conditioner, and the backseat windows are jammed in the sealed position. Jacob turns on the tape deck, a little cheer here, please. Peter, Paul, and Mary sing about lemons, a dragon puffs and swims in the sea. Every time we hit a bump my insides sear with pain. "Drive slower," I cry to Jacob, who complies.

I did not realize, until now, how harsh the surgery

really was. I can feel every jar, every rut in the road. "Slower," I plead as we go over the grated top of a sewer.

I am sitting in the back with the baby. The baby likes the loud, mufflerless motor. She's sleeping with her mouth slack. "At least the baby's happy," I gasp. "How could every tiny bump hurt so much?" I ask.

"They cut you up," Jacob says from the front seat. "They cut you right up. They took your uterus out of your body and put it on the table next to you."

"They did not," I say. "That's impossible."

"I've never seen anything like it," Jacob says, and his voice sounds a little shocked, and I realize the birth hurt him too, in a way. "They just pulled your womb out, it was blue, and they scrubbed it with a sponge and then put it on the table."

I am quiet for a moment, thinking about this. "Did they put it back?" I finally say.

"I'm sure they did," he says.

I press my lower belly. It's hollow. I am suddenly convinced it's wombless.

"But you didn't see them put it back," I say.

"That's not the kind of thing they forget," he says.

I think some more. I am perturbed, confused, extremely hot. My body sweats freely, vigorously, water pooling on the plastic car seats.

"How could they take out my uterus," I say, "and put it on the table? You mean to say it's not attached somehow? By some sort of string, a tendon? Your body parts don't just float around, do they?"

"I don't know," Jacob says. "I think they do."

I am very upset by this news. There is nothing to tether my organs in place. There are no strings here, no blue and bloody roots. I picture my liver floating up to my heart, my kidneys tipping like toy ships, and more. I picture my house, the house to which we are returning, as a most unstable place; the chairs are drifting toward the ceiling; the lamps bob along in midair. I don't want to go there. What awaits us there?

The car hits another bump. "Slower! Slower!" I scream.

Like this we inch our way forward, slower and slower, all hesitance and bruise.

I talk as though I know, but I don't. I received respectable grades in neuropsychology, in psychophysiology, even in statistics, where I had to work like an ox to grasp even the lowliest concepts—mean, median, mode. I am good at jargon, which may be why I got through graduate school in record time. "That patient? I'd say her obsessive symptomatology is secondary to her ego syntonic anorexic psychopathology, further complicated by very poor premorbid functioning, which makes her prognosis questionable." For this, in graduate school, you get accolades.

I talk as though I know, but I don't. I don't know even the simplest things. For instance, what exactly is a hormone? Yes, hormones are sex steroids with carbon rings that act upon cell clusters to decrease, increase, or stabilize mood states. That tells me nothing, and you neither.

Is a hormone wet or dry? Is it clear or colorful? Does it squirt or sprinkle? I can talk all about hormones, but I wouldn't know one if I saw it.

And genes. What about genes? They are germ cells strung along the sides of chromosomes. The X chromosome has more than four thousand genes lit up along its braided flanks, while the Y chromosome, impoverished and insecure, has a mere two or three dozen. Genes are small but superiorly powerful pieces of protein. They contain the code that causes our hair to grow, or not; they put the ocean in our eyes, make our noses aquiline; they give us complex minds, five fingers, a capacity for math, or love.

And yet, what *is* a gene? I could write a short paper on its characteristics, but grasp it, not at all. How is it, exactly, that a microscopic bulb could *cause* love? Or math? Scientists assure us that the female primate is genetically imprinted for maternity. Technically speaking, this means that on every X chromosome in every cell of her body there is a light that switches on and sends signals cascading through her flesh when the infant is near. Okay. So where. Are. The signals? Left? Right? Up? Down? The baby sleeps, her mouth slack, dribble collecting in a corner of her lower lip. I should wipe it away. Wipe it away, Lauren. I don't. Instead I think about my genes. I think about my X, all my X's, Xed out, extinct, wiped away, you're gone. The X seems eerie to me, negative capability, an existential minefield, no place for a baby to be. I am counting on my genes to get me through this. I believe what primatologists say.

I am well read, well educated, post-enlightenment, post-modern, postfeminist, postpartum. Sit back. Let the body swoop you along in the chemical current called love.

But what does love look like? What kind of chemical causes it? Is it wet, dry, sprinkled, sprayed? Could you lick it, smear it, taste it, wear it?

In some elemental and utterly essentialist sense, I have never seen love. This makes me nervous, new mother that I am. I want love in a test tube, all labeled and blue.

Then again, maybe I have seen love. The dogs are ecstatic. We let them sniff the baby, kiss us hello.

The stairs creak and I look up. There is a fat girl standing there in pedal pushers. "This is Emily," Jacob says.

"You're the live-in?" I say. I must say it rudely because Emily's face turns red and Jacob shakes his head.

"Yes," she says.

"I thought your name was Amanda," I say, thinking back to the girl we interviewed by phone months ago.

"I told you," Jacob says, "Amanda had to cancel. The agency sent Emily in her place."

"Right," I say, "I remember," although I do not, and this girl is really a shock. She comes down the stairs slowly, more like a creature than like a human, her face rutted with acne, Darth Vader on her T-shirt, and then, when she is standing closer to me, I see her tattoo.

Technically speaking, I have nothing against tattoos. However, hers is inscribed on her neck, right across the carotid artery, a flaming orange butterfly that beats, I imagine, in time with her heart. I stare and stare at the tattoo, and as I do I think I see it move, the wings pulsing ever so slightly, the inked insect coming alive.

"So you're all moved in?" I say, I squeak. I feel tears, and immediately I know the truth. Emily will be a challenge bigger than the baby. We should fire her on the spot.

Instead, I sit down. The dogs follow me, thrilled by their new little sister. "Will you get the baby away from the dogs?" Jacob barks. I should never have married him. I am fundamentally alone in the world, an X on every exiled cell in my body; while the lamps bob and the furniture drifts, I start to cry. I am postpartum, either weepy or crazy, that remains to be seen. As soon as the tears come, though, I know I cannot fire Emily, despite her T-shirt and her tattoo. She is all I have right now, my twelve-thousand-dollar middle-class ticket out of this mess, the reason I will not have to devote every moment of the next year to bottle washings and burpings, the reason I will be able to go back to work in one week, I swear I will. "I'm sorry," I say, handing the baby to Jacob and looking up at Emily. "I'm sorry I'm crying," I say. "It's nice to meet you."

"All women cry after they've had a baby," Emily says. She speaks with an accent, something south or west. She couldn't be more than twenty.

"So I've heard," I say.

"It's a big deal," she says. "You've had the baby inside you for nine months, and now that it's out, you miss it a lot. That's why women cry."

Well, this is a charming theory, even though in my case it's so patently wrong. Still, she deserves a smile for such a sweet theory. I mean that. I smile at her.

We go upstairs then, all four of us, and into the newly appointed nursery. I start to cry again. In here, it's just so hot. It is an oven; you could fry an egg on the floor. You could pluck a tiny human egg from the ovarian pod, crack it open, and fry it frilly and dead. I shiver, despite the heat.

The baby wakes up, screams. Jacob jiggles her. We all stand there and sweat.

"Maybe we should change her," I say.

"Maybe we should feed her," Jacob says.

"She might need a nap," Emily says.

We all three stand there, looking at each other. The baby screams again, then stops. In the silence, I can hear the clock ticking, ticking, ticking. I've no idea what to do. We can change her, feed her, then what? Change her, feed her again. And again. Is this maternity, no matter what your income level, a never-ending ever-present series of repetitions, an eternal fatiguing now?

That night, we eat our first dinner together, the baby in the car seat, Emily, Jacob, and I around the table. Emily tells us about her hometown of Pocatello, Idaho; she tells us she loves dragons, unicorns, tarot cards, and castles. She is an expert on fish—she has brought her aquarium with her, she hopes we don't mind, it's in her room—and she speaks at length about salt water, fresh water, the Japanese fighter versus the quiescent orange carp, and as she speaks I start to listen to the lilting twang in her voice.

After dinner, the baby and I go up to her room. I want to see the aquarium. Emily lowers the lights, and the fish spread their striped tails and glide through the lit liquid sky. "It's beautiful," I say, and I mean it.

We watch the aquarium for a while, and then Eva, in my arms, awakens. Emily has the bottle ready. The baby does what babies will do—a very simple story here—she squawks and mewls, and I sway with her in time to the drifting fish, but the baby starts to cry only harder, and harder, and Emily takes her from me, fool that I am, I don't know. How.

"Like this," Emily says, and she brings the baby right up against her and rocks from side to side, all the while patting her back very fast, very firm, I watch. The baby starts to quiet, something about the hand-foot combo I think, and Emily begins to sing:

> *Ob-la-di ob-la-da*
> *Life goes on bra*

and inside of me I feel a kind of quieting too. I see that the butterfly on our nanny's neck is not a butterfly but a tropical fish, its fins spread, swimming. Swimming. We are swimming now, and it occurs to me that this might be what love looks like, not a chemical so much as a certain sort of stroke, a song, multicolored, wet as water, dry like flesh, hand and foot, many-limbed, rocked and rocking, that girl, she sings us both to sleep.

June 16

There is no dust. The next morning I come downstairs to no dust, to curtains cleaned and smelling of soap. Light fills the kitchen, where each teacup dangles from a little gold hook. I stare and stare. Someone has cleaned here, Emily. She offers me a seat.

I sit. The baby is next to me, in a bassinet covered with a netting of cream pastille. With the windows open, the netting tosses on a tongue of fresh air.

The one emotion I never expected to feel at any point so soon after my baby's birth is calm, but here it is, ushered in, perhaps, by the clean kitchen, the stacked tea towels, by the medicine cabinet—this girl is a godsend—which I open to bottles arranged according to size. I touch cotton balls. I tap four Prozac into my palm. I take them with a crisp glass of cider poured over crackling ice.

Every morning for much of my pregnancy I threw up quickly, efficiently, miserably, and then ate a single Carr's cracker washed down with ginger ale. I grew accustomed to the nausea; it was as unremarkable as putting on a pair of socks, or as the foamy toothpaste that followed its bitter spurt. Nausea during pregnancy never bothered me. I had, it seemed, more momentous worries.

Nevertheless, its sudden absence is startling. I drink the cider—no nausea. For the first time in seven months I take my first sip of coffee, criminal, how good it is. The baby sleeps sweetly in her blankets. She is no trouble.

June 20

This odd calmness, this *neutrality*. Where's the breakdown everyone promised me? Or, at the very least, where's the intensity of emotion? It is surreal, anticlimactic. Perhaps it is because Emily keeps the house so clean. Perhaps it's because the baby seems barely born; she sleeps and sleeps and sleeps, she is no trouble. She sleeps four hours at a time in the night, sometimes more; we have to wake her, feed her, and then she slips back with milk on her mouth. "Is she sick," I say to Jacob, "or just lazy?"

"She's a baby," he says to me, "she's fine."

She's fine, of course she's fine, the pediatrician says she's fine, I will not worry. And really, mostly, I don't worry, because her skin is Maybelline pink and her breath sounds steady. So what is the story here? What does motherhood mean? So far, all I can say is this. Whatever you plan for, it will not happen. You plan for your labor but the baby is breach. You plan to call her Sara but she comes out all Kate, what with those Irish blue eyes. I planned for a crisis and instead I get calmness, which confounds the story, this narrative of mother becoming eluding me, slipping out from under me, the plot points won't cohere. I have little love, little care, no craziness, a girl named Eva, a baby born but unborn, sleeping still, with these I will try to tell the tale.

June 30

Today the baby spoke! I know this is impossible, but I heard it with my own sane ears. I was sitting on the couch, she across the room in her bassinet, I couldn't see her, but suddenly, from deep in its hollows, a very clear, simple, singular word—*icy,* she said. Icy? Icy? I went over to her. Her eyes were wide open, and she looked up at me, a gaze fixed, intense, and ever so slightly accusing.

July 5

I am recovering. Inside me jazzed up cells speed toward recovery, the cesarean slit going from vicious crimson to vaginal pink, the welter of black stitching melting back into my belly. When I stand in front of the mirror, I can see how I was pregnant, but already my breasts have become more modest, the veins now pale stroke marks, that's it. The doctors told me it would take weeks to heal from the surgery. In a cesarean, they cut through layers and layers of muscle and skin, peeling you back like baklava and reaching deep into the viscera. "It will take weeks," they said. "Don't lift. Don't drive. Don't push yourself."

Truth is, I feel fine. Or nearly fine. The body heals aggressively. The dark line running from navel to pubis is gone. The Indian markings at the edges of my face, also eradicated—hello, old face. Last night in the shower, when I washed my breasts, the aureoles shed the tan paint of pregnancy, flaking off in my fingers, the pale flesh color coming back. I looked at my hands, flecked. I held them under the spray. The brown bits drained away, and I stepped out, newly clean.

What I mean to say is this: I am a mother, but I don't look like a mother. I don't feel like a mother. Over and over during the day, or at night when I watch her sleep, I whisper, *"I am a mother, mother, mother,"* as I did when I was pregnant, and I've grown accustomed to the word, but it stays at a distance from me. I thought I would be smashed flat, or heaved high, mythically altered for this, the most mythic of roles but, shock of all shock, here I am, still me. And the baby? I have come to like her a little bit. That's it. A little bit.

July 9

It must be because of the schedule. Which works as follows. Emily has Eva from 7:00 A.M. to 1:00 P.M. I have her from 1:00 P.M. to 7:00 P.M. Jacob has her from 7:00 P.M. to 11:00 P.M., and we share the night feedings. Think about this. There are twenty-four hours in a day, and I spend only one-quarter of those as a mother. Three-quarters of my time is still . . . my time. Twelve thousand dollars a year buys you not only a room of your own but a self of your own. A long time ago my sister said to me, "Fatherhood is something you do. Motherhood is something you are." But I have learned that's not necessarily true. Tonight I had dinner with a friend. What a meal! We splurged on rare hamburgers and steak fries. For dessert I had mousse in a tall cup with a long, ladylike spoon, the sort of spoon a spinster might have in her silver collection, delicate scrollwork pressed into its curved handle. I held the spoon. I ate the meat and chocolate, and it was only when I rose to go that I remembered I had a baby—*I have a baby*—how odd, that she can recede from me, leaving me whole moments when I am solely, utterly singular, when I have my hands right here, my heart, right here—

Still sane.

July 25

"How is Jacob handling it?" my friend Elizabeth asks. "Has he come through?"

Oh yes, he has. Fatherhood, it appears, is something you are. Motherhood is something you do. He is transformed by a passion that leaves me a little jealous. "Don't forget," I say to him, "don't forget I'm the one you married. Not Eva. Eva's going to grow up, grow away from us, but you're stuck with me for life."

"I know that," he says as he dances with her.

"Stop dancing with her!" I say.

He doesn't. He rushes home from work. He spends long hours reading her the Bhagavad-Gita. "She can't understand that," I say. "Of course she can," he says. Inside me I say, "Read to me, to me, to me," and a loneliness that is not illness floats up, cloaks me; sometimes it is dark. Sometimes I feel younger and younger, and I can see my hands, so small, who will hold them? Having a child does not change you so much as amplify whatever is unresolved. I am a child and I have a child. I am a mother without a mother.

July 31

Quote: *My children cause me the most exquisite suffering of which I have any experience. It is the suffering of ambivalence, the murderous alternation between bitter resentment and raw-edged nerves, and blissful gratification and tenderness. . . . There are times when I feel only death will free us from one another, when I envy the barren woman who has the luxury of her regrets, but lives a life of privacy and freedom.*

Adrienne Rich, *Of Woman Born: Motherhood as Experience and Institution*

Quote: *Ariel: I imagine all the ways I can kill you. I can drown you in the bathtub. I can smother you with a pillow. I can bang your head on the floor, once, hard. Last month I wept when I heard about a baby dying. This month I do the killing. I kill, and tremble with horror. Why such images?*

Phyllis Chesler, *With Child, A Diary of Motherhood*

Quote: *With good preparation and reasonable help, you may find the post partum period to be deeply meaningful, even ecstatic. You may feel at one with the entire universe and flooded with love for your new baby, especially when you look at your sleeping infant.*

Elisabeth Bing, *Laughter and Tears: The Emotional Life of New Mothers*

I read these words and feel rage. The rage is not toward my baby but toward the women, the whole godawful lot of them, who have made the myth of motherhood, even as they've tried to dismantle it. I understand their impulses, to free maternity from its sweet tethers, but in doing so they've created yet another story that panicked me throughout my pregnancy and may not reflect the reality for all women. Theirs is a story of blood whisperings and dark urges, of bitter anger in the throat that then gives way to ecstasy. The story of motherhood that I can find nowhere exists on neither pole but somewhere in the banal place between extremes where like precedes love, where the self, if it is altered at all, goes so gradually it leaves only the palest trace. My friend Elena, who has a two-year-old and who also has hired child-care help (85 percent of families in this country utilize some type of full- or part-time child care), says, "Isn't this the hardest thing you've ever done? Aren't you just always overwhelmed?" and I say, "No. Having a baby is sort of like having a bipedal pet. Except with a pet you can't really hire help, so maybe a baby's easier."

She looks at me aghast. She looks angry. "I'm sorry," I say. Motherhood's biggest taboo may be not rage but mildness. Mother love must be intense. I am not intense.

I feel a great guilt.

So far, it is only my guilt that makes me a mother.

August 10

Two months old. Sixty days you've been on this earth. Do you dream of the womb, its red haze and watery thumps? I lie next to you on the bed. We are a perfect picture: naked baby, naked mother, window open, and the thick heat of a lazy August day. I trace the creased knob of your umbilicus, the rise of knees. I put my teeth to your cheek and see how the slightest pressure makes a mark that fades so fast it seems my mouth was never there. I bring you close to me, Eva, and try to call you mine. You are definite, separate; love cannot be willed. On your lids are two bright marks. "What are they?" I asked your doctor. "They're called stork bites," she said to me. "Newborns sometimes have pinched red places, like they've been carried in a bird's beak, hence the name."

Hence, the name. I lie close to you, in a warm wind. Outside, a car is having trouble, and the smell of oil rises into the room. I look at you here, but I see you there, high up, carried by a creature that is not me. I see you story-book, magical, rarely real. You sleep so well. When will you wake up? When will I wake up? I see you in the sky,

Eva, against a blue background, someone else's perfect picture, click click.

And then the shutter, closed.

August 11

When birth by cesarean section deprives first-time mothers of the experience of giving birth, they make even worse mothers. Only 3 percent of primiparous monkeys whose first infant was delivered by cesarean section even picked the baby up off the floor of the cage. They were far more interested in lapping up the addictive chemicals from the birth fluids that keepers had smeared on the baby than in the newborn itself.

       Sarah Blaffer Hrdy, *Mother Nature: Maternal Instincts and How They Shape the Human Species*

August 12

To: Aprildoss@mindspring.com
From: Lauren@channel1.com
Subject: Post Partum
cc:
bcc:
attachments

My name is Lauren Slater. I saw your posting on Parents.com FAQ's, and thought I might write to you personally because, it seems, we have some significant things in common. I, too, am a psychologist. I, too, have struggled with significant mental illness, although, when I got pregnant, I had been relatively symptom free for ten years. The pregnancy, however, was brutal for me, well, not the whole pregnancy, but the first fifteen weeks or so, when I was decimated by a depression that my doctors said was largely due to the surge in progesterone levels. From your posting I gather that you too had very significant antenatal psychiatric issues. I was told, given my antenatal antics, that I was almost guaranteed to have significant postpartum problems, and it would not be too much to say how shocked (and cautiously thrilled) I am that this has not yet happened. I'm wondering whether you have had any ppd and, if so, at what point in the postpartum period it occurred. I'm also wondering whether your baby is okay. You said you took psych drugs during your pregnancy: which ones? I took Prozac, 120 mg, lithium, 450 mg, and Klonopin, 1 mg. My baby's name is Eva. She sleeps and sleeps, sucks down milk (not nursing, the drugs), and then nods off again. I'm sure many parents would say I'm lucky to have such an easy baby, and the doctor tells me not to worry, but I do. For instance, she appears to have little muscle tone. Sometimes she does this weird shudder, almost like a small seizure. I told her ped about this but the ped can't tell what I'm talking about. "Just watch her for a while," I say, but Eva never does it in the doctor's office.

Anyway, I'm sure that's a lot more than you wanted to hear. I'd appreciate, if you have the time, knowing how your baby is, and how you are, but if you don't have the time, I of course understand, and wish you well.

Best,

Lauren Slater

August 16

Going back to work today. The clinic is located in a poor section of town, a place where the rusted carcasses of cars hulk in the narrow streets, and the stop signs hang from only one hook, crooked and unsure. It's easy to ignore the stop signs, their command tilted like a question mark; I drive through, in my truck.

A siren wails. I look in my rearview. The stop sign is behind me now, unheeded. The red bulb on top of the tiny cop car spins and spins; it's so hysterical, *calm down*, I want to say. The police car nudges at the truck's bumper, and I tingle deep down in my body. The siren screams. The sun shines. I have two choices, pull over, or floor it. Why I think about gunning my truck down the side streets of the inner city is not quite clear to me, we're talking about just a ticket, after all, but I can feel that police car in my body, those men tapping at my pelvis, and it seems wrong, and it seems gleeful, how I, as a *mother*, might also be a fugitive, a criminal, and, in doing so, rewrite the whole damn word—*mother*, which, without the *m*, means "other, outside"—I need not be trapped in a label. I can create this, write this, defy this, and the siren spins cherry, spins silly.

So I do it. I gun it. The truck lurches forward, and in my rearview mirror I see the cartoon faces of the cops go all surprised. *Some guy,* they think, *some punk in a pickup, okay.*

My heart is hammering. My cesarean slit has come alive, itching, suddenly scarlet with pain. Perhaps the postpartum crisis is starting. I laugh. I hear my laugh, *heh heh,* and then it stops. I am silent. I glide to the curb, roll down my window, and lean out, black hair blowing in the wind, the little lace collar around my dress sparkling white in the summer sunlight. I smile.

Cop 1 comes over. He's in long blue polyester jodhpurs, with a silver star on his shirt. I long to touch the star, it seems so festive. "Hello," he says.

"Hi," I say. I touch my lace collar, drawing attention to it. This is bad, I know, I'm supposed to be a feminist, but truth is, this will be my seventh moving violation in three years, and I'm going to do what I can to get out of it.

"License?" he says.

Excellent. It just happens to be that my license is located in a very floral upholstered wallet, which I make a great show of pulling from the ladylike pouch of my pocketbook. The cop squints at me. He looks from me to my truck, back to me, clearly befuddled. I smile at him. People have told me I have a charming, almost elfin smile, let's hope they're right.

I give him my little laminated license. He looks at it and

gives it back. Then, like he's a horse, he sticks his neck way, way into my car, and sniffs around. Is he sniffing me? I press myself back against the seat. He looks at the tossed off containers, the coffee cups with dried brown lip marks on their rims, the defunct air freshener shaped like something spiked, lying desiccated on the floor. There is a lot of gravel in my truck. Then he looks at the car seat.

"Car seat," he says. He seems to still be sniffing, even as he speaks.

"I know," I say. "I just had a baby. This is her car seat." I touch the plastic hull strapped in backward.

"Against the law," he says.

"What's against the law?" I say.

"You can't have a car seat in the front seat," he says. "That's against the law."

"Well," I say, and now I'm growing irritated, "as you can see this is a truck, and it doesn't have a backseat, so my only other option would be to put the car seat in the pickup part, or on the roof."

"Car seat," he says again, he seems to be stuck.

"What would you suggest I do?" I say. "Do you mean to tell me a mother is not allowed to transport her child in the vehicle of her choice?"

"You can't have a car seat in the front seat," he says.

"Do you mean to tell me," I say, "that the law requires a truck-owning mother to buy a new car? I would need to see that in writing."

Understand, I say all of this nicely.

Suddenly, the policeman sighs. He leans on his elbows

in my open window and rubs sweat from his eyes. He seems exhausted, defeated, depressed. He shakes his head. "Are you okay?" I ask.

"Sure," he says. "You live around here?"

"I work up the street," I say. "I'm a psychologist."

"Really?" he says. "You see a lot of loonies?"

"All the time," I say. We nod to each other conspiratorially.

"I'll have to see your registration," he says. "You ran the stop sign back there."

"Did I?" I say. "I didn't even see a stop sign."

I open my glove compartment and pull out my registration. This is when it happens. I see something strange in there, something glossy and discolored, I will not look. He writes me out a warning. "Take care of the loonies," he says as he walks back to his car. He drives away. I am alone on a side street deep in the inner city. A torn American flag shudders on its pole, and is then still. A dalmatian whines pitifully at a broken bulkhead, scratching to get in. Slowly, I reach over to the glossy thing in the glove compartment and take it out. I know what it is. But I act as though I don't. I take it out, Eva's ultrasound picture at thirty-two weeks gestation. The heat has ruined it, the colors merged and bleeding, her hands a bruised blue, her head hot red and messy.

"Warning," my citation reads. I put both the citation and the ultrasound back in the glove compartment. I keep picturing her head, hot red and messy. Warning. Warning. I drive to work slowly, humbled, obeying every sign I see.

August 17

Eva screams. Her face is full of blood. She twists on her wrappings, and when I pick her up she arches, hissing, her tongue a single moving muscle, in and out, in and out. "Eva, Eva Eva," I say. I am gone from her now ten hours a day. I am back at work full-time. I have her red-hot head in my car. I have a warning.

"Let me try," says Jacob. He takes her from me. No go. Her neck is such a useless stalk. She flops and heaves. A jet of milky bile spurts from her mouth.

"Is she okay?" I ask.

We rock her. We talk to her. We blow up a huge yellow beach ball, sit on it, and bounce, and bounce, until the sun goes down and the sky gets gray. Still our baby screams. Her stomach hurts. We force a dropper in her mouth, gas relief. She gags it up. In the darkened room, the yellow ball glows, full of fury. Our Eva is full of fury. Suddenly she has changed. She has woken up. She knows, you see. She knows what I have done to her red-hot head.

August 18

The doctor says it might be colic. We switched formulas. The new formula is pulverized chalk, mixed with strained water, leaving clumps behind in the bottle. Jacob glares at me. The baby howls. "This stuff is shit," he says.

"Formula is shit," he says, and, because I can't, or won't, breast-feed, I don't know what to say.

I take a wire whisk out of the drawer and try to dissolve the clumps. The baby's cries jangle us. It is 3:00 A.M., owl time, bat time, time for the breeding of black cats. Where is Emily? I wish she were here to help. The clumps are stubborn, more like barnacles. Jacob starts to shake. "We can't feed her this," he says.

"We have to," I say.

He storms down to the cellar, comes back up carrying a test tube and a beaker. He makes a new bottle, measuring out the powder with his perfect chemist hand, adding water just so. He can do it. I can't. He goes to feed the baby. Sometimes, I think, he hates me. "No," I say. "No."

"No what," he says.

"I want to feed the baby," I say. Something in my voice, perhaps, some intensity he has not heard before. He gives her to me. Her cries are rips and pins, they get into the uterine wound and make me shiver. I have to hold the baby. Suddenly it is not she who needs me, but I who need her. Don't ask me to explain, I can't. I can. We are creatures who must give comfort. We ache to give comfort, to heal what hurts. The baby. My baby. She takes the nipple whole, her cheeks collapsing inward, her lids lazing down. The colic is making me a mother.

To: Lauren@channel1.com
From: Aprildoss@mindspring.com
Subject: postpartum

cc:
bcc:
attachments

Dear Lauren,

Glad to get your e-mail. Pregnancy was hell for me, and, surprise of all surprise, I also don't have any postpartum difficulties. My baby's name is Derrick. Derrick was my brother's name. He killed himself two years ago. Manic depression runs through my family tree. Before I got pregnant I went off all my drugs (Depakote for mania, Prozac for depression) and took major amounts of folic acid to clean out my system. I made it for about two months and then crashed horribly. I just couldn't do it, maybe like you? So I went back on, at my psychiatrist's insistence. I was hospitalized while they stabilized me.

I feel that Derrick developed in a toxic minefield. Because your blood volume doubles in pregnancy, the amount of drugs that worked for you before doesn't work when you're carrying, so I had to triple my dose, same exact as yours, 120 mg of Prozac, enough to launch a rocket. Like your Eva, my Derrick seems almost perfect but it's hard to look at him without imagining a little Chernobyl in my uterus. I feel very bad, but I also feel I had no choice. Mental illness is not a choice. It killed my brother. I don't want it to kill me.

Both my husband and I think Derrick is the eighth wonder of the world. Developmentally so far he seems normal. He is just learning to hold his head up. He gurgles. The only problem is this. He has an extra crease on his right palm, a very insignificant birth defect, except that no one knows what it means.

I run to Eva. For a mild mother, I move fast. Emily is holding her. I bend over the baby and unwrap her palm, but Eva swats at me, there is something she does not want me to see.

August 25

This is what I do. We are creatures bred to give comfort. Water rumbles in the tub. Blue sticky stars waver on the bottom of the chrome bed. I lay Eva on the plush bath mat, she is naked. I am naked. I unwrap a cake of white soap and then slowly, so slowly, lower us in. She screams, the tiny multiple muscles in her stomach clenched. As soon as she touches the wet warmth, she stills, her body loosens, her eyelids drop down. Under her half-closed lids her irises move; her tiny mouth flutters. I sit in the tub and watch her. I wash her with the white soap. Now I know all that a moment might be.

August 26

"Do you feel like a mother?" my sister asks me.
"I don't think so," I say. "I'm not sure."

"Well, do you feel like an aunt?" my sister says. "Before Eva was born you said you wanted to be her aunt."

"No, not an aunt," I say. "I don't feel like her aunt."

"Well, what is it that you feel?" my sister asks.

I search in my head. I see the cake of white soap, the clumpy formula, my husband with the test tubes, the tiny buttocks snug in my palms. "I feel like a woman," I say slowly, "who is taking care of a child."

How slowly we grow.

August 27

Eva is twelve. She has curly black hair and fizz green eyes. Standing on tiptoes, she reaches up, pulls a book down from the shelf. "Why did you write about me?" she says.

"I was," I say, "trying to write about love, how it happened."

"How did it happen?" she says. "What was it that made you love me?"

"It was just . . . you," I say. I am at a loss for words.

"I want to know," she says.

I think back. I think forward. You cried and cried until it hurt my heart. One day you smiled. One day you spoke. I bathed with you, in tepid water, and you touched my nipple. I had a dream that you drowned, I don't know, Eva, I can't say.

Is love a mystery?

Is it an inevitability?

Is even the most clenched heart capable of it?

Today, Eva fell and hurt her head. I walked around for hours, my own skull smacked and smarting.

Love grows like the embryo grows, without any effort from your fine mind. Love grows despite you, in the interstices of each entry, in the white space, without a word.

August 28

On assignment for *The New York Times Magazine*, I am going to interview a plastic surgeon designing wings for human beings. He lives in Vermont, far away. I pull up to his house, and three gold hens flap from a tree on his lawn. An enormous turtle sticks out his scrotum neck and flicks a swampy tongue.

The surgeon lets me in. Behind him hovers his wife. His home smells of formaldehyde, of something spoiled, and in the sunken living room snakes lie coiled in cages, their shiny throats bulging around the bodies of mice.

The surgeon takes me to his office. I have never seen anything like it. Every drawer pull is a golden ear. Bronze hands cup low-wattage bulbs, potpourri. He has a crystal ball, a beautiful piece of bubbled glass that, when you peer inside it, shows different body parts made of wax: a perfect nose, a taut breast with a fat pink nipple, someone's smile. "Patients always want to know what they will look like after surgery," he tells me. "My wife and I made them this crystal ball, and they look into it."

I look into it. When I lean to my left, the nose rises up, to my right and I see the smile. So many ways to sculpt. So many swerves in a breakable world.

We sit at his desk. He shows me his tools—clippers, pruners, scalpels, shears. He shows me a large swath of human skin pinned to his wall, removed from the armpit of an old lady. "Touch it," he says. I do. The skin is crinkled, and there are visible pores where her hairs once were.

"I am," says the surgeon, "especially interested in hands. When the human hand is deformed it usually means there's a corollary deformity in the heart. That's because the hand and the heart form in the embryo at roughly the same time, seven weeks gestation."

I nod. I feel a little something in my throat. It is dry, like a stone or a stopper.

"So," says the surgeon, "you can tell a lot about a person from his hands." He takes out many colored photographs. They show what the possibilities are. In one photograph the hand has only two long talons. In another, the child's hand is twisted like a vicious corkscrew, each nail a black bruise. "If it's the left hand," he says, "then the left heart chamber is probably bad too. Vice versa for the right."

What can I say? My own hands hurt. I feel them clenching up, cold.

"You look a little wan," the surgeon says.

"No," I say.

"Plastic surgery," he says, "is different from any other field of medicine in that it's not about what is. It's about what will be, what could be. We are about the future. We are about philosophy and pushing the limits of what's acceptable. For instance, to me these hands are beautiful. A hand with four thumbs or two talons has possibilities beyond what an ordinary hand can do. In the eighteenth century," the surgeon says, "they used to believe there was very little difference between a monster and a marvel, and I'm inclined to agree."

I leave him, his voice tucked into my tape recorder. He has shown me his drawings of wings, beautiful and ridiculous, Icaruses floating, taut flesh stretched in gliders from wrist to hip. "In twenty years," he says, "we'll see these wings. People will want them like an accessory, like a punk haircut. Mark my words."

But for now, driving back, the only thing that flies is my mind, filled with turning, scraping, tiny human hands. And then above me a V of dark loons heading into a cave of purplish cloud. Autumn is coming. A storm is coming. The pavement on the road turns damp and dark, and even though we speed, the world stays still, waiting for its clouds to crack.

I drive along. Rain comes down, darting silver and sideways. Leaves whoosh from trees. Exits loom up, fade back, and even after hours pass I am no closer to home. I start to cry.

"Go backwards," a man says. He is wiping down a dirty counter in a diner. A waitress has a bright, smeared mouth. A cigarette smokes in an ashtray, its long, soft ash building, something to touch.

When I finally pull into the driveway, it's nine at night. Three times I have stopped on the road to call Jacob and tell him I'm lost, and three times there's been no answer. However, he is home. The house is lit up, six yellow squares in the storm.

"Where were you?" he says. "I'm tired," he says, and indeed he is, playing dad all day, going to work all week, there is little loose time anymore. Each second is accounted for. There is not so much a strain as a serious separation between us, one that started with conception, widened with my belly, and continues with the presence of the baby. We practice what I call tag team parenting. While one of us is on shift, the other is pursuing the old life. This brings freedom, and great gaps. We are rarely together anymore.

I hug him. He hugs me back, but his arms feel unconvincing. "What's wrong?" I say. He does not answer.

I go to Eva's room. She's asleep, but Jacob has left the little lamp burning. It is my favorite lamp, a pink marble base and a spray-painted gold shade with cardboard cutouts shadowing stars and moons on the walls. In this galaxy, in this time, under the light of this little lamp, I look at my daughter's sleeping hands. I count all the creases, trace her life lines, move my finger through a future at once tactile and invisible. I feel a field, a boy with a denim notebook. I feel a dog named Nelson, a house in Mexico, and a rope. She cries once but lets me keep her hand, and I can see by the light of this little lamp how well formed it is, correct in every crease. I think about monsters and marvels, bodies placed at the outermost poles, where they astound us in their strange specifics; not her. She is not there, on those poles, in that weird weather. I suddenly know it to be true. She is here, a girl named Eva, ten pounds, milk on her mouth; her troubles will be of the ordinary, aching kind—lost loves, crumpled meanings. No more. No less. I suddenly know it to be true, and maybe that disappoints more than it relieves. Yesterday, a friend of mine called Eva pleasant, *pleasant*, and I was offended. This girl will defy me, I who have always honored, even needed, the extremes. Eva. Average girl. Mean.

August 30

"I'm tired," says Jacob.

"I'm tired too," I say.

"I get up with her at least five times a week," he says, "while you sleep."

"That's not true," I say, "it's half and half."

"I'm working so many hours," he says.

"Maybe we should let her cry it out, train her to sleep through."

"That's barbaric," he says.

"Are you calling me barbaric?" I say.

"Don't be so snappy," he says.

Meanwhile, he is cutting carrots for a stew. We argue all the time now. We should feed her this. We should feed her that. We should let her cry. We should go to comfort.

Chop chop chop. He is cutting carrots. Bright orange chips. Something simmers.

September 11

Still sane.

September 12

It has come to the point where I cannot listen to Eva cry unless she is crying in my arms. I suppose this is a form of love, but not the kind I would most wish for. It is instinctual, biological, love on a cellular level. Intimacy, I am coming to understand, is corporeal. It has to do with the distance between bodies. I wish for more. I wish for a passion that transcends space. When I am with Eva, she is my heart. When I am gone from her, at work, or with a friend, she ceases to exist.

September 25

The trees are rash red. The dogs have more or less adjusted. The baby is asleep. Later on, she will wake up and I will go to her, or Jacob will go to her, and the odd one out will pass the night alone. Once, we were two points that formed a line. Now we are three points in a triangle, someone high up on the tip, standing separate.

"You know," I say to Jacob. We are sitting in our bedroom. We are both exhausted, at the end of a long day. "You know," I say, "it's been three and a half months, and look at me, I'm fine. The doctors were wrong. I feel so lucky," I say, "to be surrounded by so much love."

"You are lucky," he says. "You have a lot of things to love."

"My dogs," I say, "and Eva."

"And no one else?" he says.

I make my voice twangy, western, silly. "And a certain man," I sing, "who once loved me."

"I still love you," he says.

"I hope so," I say, "because now, with a kid, it would be really hard to get a divorce."

"But not impossible," he says, his voice soft.

I don't look at him. I hug the dog hard. "You want a divorce," I say. I don't ask it; I say it, my voice leaden.

"No," he says, unconvincingly.

"I would never," I say, and my voice turns fierce, "I would never give you Eva."

"You might not have a choice," he says.

I cannot quite believe where we so suddenly are. Three minutes ago we were in our bedroom, a little cranky, very tired. Suddenly, the seas have shifted and we drop deep, and deeper still. When you birth a baby, you birth a new capacity for cruelty, this is the surprise.

"What's that supposed to mean?" I say.

He blinks once, twice. I touch my head. We want, I can tell, we both want to back up, back out, but we can't; the undertow, the tiredness, the human need to push right into the heart of the wound.

"The courts wouldn't necessarily favor you," he says. He blinks again, surprised. Shocked, we both are.

"I mean," he continues, and we both know what he's going to say before he says it. "I could bring up your illnesses," he says, he almost whispers, "if I had to. The courts would never let a child go with you."

"Fuck you," I say.

"Okay," he says.

"I could bring up your illegal drugs," I say. "I could bring up the fact that you do illegal drugs. What do you think Your Honor would say to that?"

We go on. We cannot stop. We are explorers, giddy and sickened by this new terrain, how hard we can suddenly hurt each other, how much power and terror there is. Being. A. Parent. Stop. I want to stop now.

Jacob touches me on the arm. "This is awful," he says.

"What's happening to us?" I say.

"We had a baby," he says.

"Will we recover?" I say.

And then we lie together for a long time. He strokes my hair. The dogs watch us, their eyes slitted with suspicion.

October 15

"So," says my sister. "Do you feel like a mother yet?"
I surprise myself by saying yes.
"Cool," says my sister. "When did this happen?"
"I don't know," I say. "Last Tuesday maybe?"
When did this happen? I wanted to chart love, to code it or encrypt it. Love = proximity + time. Love = oxytocin + night feedings. But in the end, I'm no closer to understanding it, even when I feel it.
"Look," says my sister, "this is a *story* you're trying to tell. Every story needs a revelation."

Revelation

I am still here. My name, for instance, is still my name. I crossed the great divide only to find I still like hamburgers with brilliant spatters of mustard, love to browse in bookstores late on Saturday nights, to write in the quiet of my study when either Emily or Jacob is on duty. Becoming a mother if—and this is a critical if—you have enough money for help does not mean stripping the membranes and being born anew; it means a series of tiny innumerable tasks added to your life that in the short run mean little but in the long run amount to something. It means coming home from work two hours earlier than you did before because that's when the sitter gets off. It means cooking dinners every night because, after all, you don't have just yourself to feed, or not. It means learning about couscous, high-iron rice, organic spinach, nontoxic pots, things you never thought of, little addendums to your brain, insignificant in isolation but, collectively, it takes up space. Being a mother means going to the pet store for three hours on Sundays so your girl can see the birds. It means learning and seeing colors anew—there's purple, there's red, say *red, red, red,* and so you see red as though for the first time, blood in the eye, brightness. Being a mother means knowing the luxuriousness of giving comfort, bringing the slack body up, holding her close; she melts into your form, which is, when all is said and done, still your form. Like so much in life, being a mother is entirely undramatic, filled with small pleasures and multiple inconveniences that only over weeks and months leave marks of any significance. You look back and say, "I know things I did not know before. I love like I did not love before, but how, or when, this happened, is really all mystery, steps of smoke." You cannot capture it. Being a mother is a lot like growing up. When, or how, did you become an adult? What was the precise moment you lost your childhood? No one can say. In fact, it's all so permeable, there are many moments, even now, when childhood comes caroming back. The

line is fragile. Our separate selves collide. We move between states of being, never fully occupying for very long
any particular one. Therefore, with Eva, there are times
when I am absolutely a mother, when I whisk off a diaper,
when I burp her like a pro, when I discuss with gusto the
merits of Graco versus EvenFlo, all the while thinking,
*How odd. A year ago this kind of conversation would have horrified
me.* Or when I grind up her food with a hand-cranked gad-
get, organic apples turning a pale mush gold; my wrists
hurt. My girl will have the best.

And yet, only hours after that, when she is asleep and I
am alone in the living room, my old, motherless imagination presses in on me, and I am spinning stories, or deep in
the dream of a book, a place utterly alone, graciously singular.

There is a line, but I cannot find it. At some point, you
cease being a child and become an adult. At some point
you cease being motherless and become a mother, but
what I didn't know was how this line is etched in smoke, a
child's chalk drawing, you go back and forth. What freedom. What luck. The language misleads us. The grammar
cannot contain the truth. There is no such concept, I think,
as *to be*, which implies an exit and an entrance, a departure
point and a reconsolidation. No. Even for the most over-
worked, impoverished, marginalized mother, no. You are
always your old self and always becoming your new self,
seesaw, past and future in a dialectical tension out of
which springs this complex, nuanced present we live in.
Now the baby cries. I will go to her. I will kiss her on the

mouth. I will rock her for minutes, maybe hours, and a pleasant muzziness will settle over this mother, the enforced quietness ensuring I see specifics—the grain of my wood floor, the blue on the black crow's wing—and then her father will come and take her and I, I think I will venture out into the night, or read deep into a book, or write a work memo, or look out the window and wait for the bats to come. They come every night in the dusk, swooping over our yard, their membranous wings stretched taut like nylon, furred black heads, diaphanous beings, fluid flight.

October 16

To: Lauren@channel1.com
From: Aprildoss@mindspring.com
Subject: Pregnancy
cc:
bcc:
attachments

So, maybe we have escaped. I'm starting my training at Mass General today. Derrick will be in day care a few days a week. I have an idea for a study. I think maybe you and I escaped ppd *because* we had such difficult, or at least thoughtful pregnancies. Here's the theory:

Current psych literature suggests a high correlation

between psychiatric difficulties and anxieties during pregnancy and a poor postpartum outcome. However, have you read Anne Oakley? *Go out and get her books.* She's a 1970s psych researcher, with excellent methodologies, but she's completely passé. What Oakley found, and this, of course, was before our cultural love affair with hormones and biochemistry, was that the higher a woman's ambivalence and distress during pregnancy, the less likely she was to have a poor postpartum outcome. In Oakley's 1970s world, when psychodynamics prevailed over chemistry, ambivalence, depression, even psychosis during pregnancy indicated a woman in preparation for her new role, and this woman, who essentially did her postpartum adjustments ahead of time, was all set psychologically by the time the baby was born. Oakley found women who were happy and excited during their pregnancies were often more shocked and let down when the real baby emerged, and it wasn't all sweetness. Antenatal depression, in other words, may be adaptive. Antenatal crisis may be preserving. Our insanity may have been, in reality, very sane.

Three cheers!

April

To: Aprildoss@mindspring.com
From: Lauren@channel1.com
Subject: pregnancy
cc:
bcc:
attachments

Hi April:

So pregnancy, what is it? At its best, maybe, it's a tool to be used, a time of active engagement, fervent imaginings, fears, little tadpole turns, cliff drops, sick stomachs, it's a rehearsal in space, in psyche. Pregnancy is time. You can use it well, and go a little crazy, or you can use it poorly, and go oblivious. Pregnancy is the ultimate betwixt and between, what Turner and van Gennep said, the liminal state. It is not for buying booties or reading What to Expect. It's not even for your body or your nausea. Pregnancy at its best occurs in the mind. It is pure thought. It is a story told all in ifs.

Grammatically, narratively, it is a hard and highly literary tale to tell. By the time you get to the end, you are just barely beginning.

Eva sends her love,

Lauren

December 21, the Solstice

Tonight is the longest night of the year. The sky is absolutely clear. Jacob says we must make time if we want to survive as a couple.

We go out for dinner. For the first time since the baby has been born, and on the longest night of the year, we go to a pub, where a gas fire burns in the grate and waiters serve tall glasses of beer.

At first, we have nothing to say. But then, we do. A child's chalk drawing. Steps of smoke. We met ten years ago, at the riverside. He told me he could read my palm, and then he did, bending over me, his red-blond beard brushing my life lines, a story rising from his sweet lips, something about dragons and beach balls and Nelson Mandela.

This is Jacob. I have known him for 10 years, 120 months, 3,652 days, 87,648 hours. We go back, before Eva, and here, without Eva, and with two salted lime margaritas, we remember this. It comes in little bits. "A river," he says. "Our wedding," I say, "the red dress I wore," and we smile. The difference is, these moments will be harder and harder to come by, finding ourselves outside the triangle, that pointed, difficult thing, its tip sharp in the air.

Tonight, we are a line again. Two points. The shortest distance. The margaritas go down. We laugh.

He explains the solar system to me.

"Will we survive as a couple," I ask, "if we only see each other alone, like, twice a year?"

"Good question," he says. He holds my hand. The salt is excellent, sharp, solid crystals. We will. We will. We do. We are not a single solid shape but multiple shifting shapes, a child's chalk drawing, a line. Love goes back and forth, before and after. "We must rely on memory," I say, "to get us through the cold times."

"The cruel times," he says. "I'm sorry."

Another margarita please.

We drink like fish. Like teenagers.

We stumble out into the glorious cold. We hold hands. It is almost Christmas; all the stores are open, and in every window colorful goods and balls are piled high, striped pillows, velvet tablecloths of deep, robust maroon, a rocking horse of tin and paint, a bright doll, a star hanging on a string.

"Let me buy you a present," Jacob says.

"That's okay," I say. "Let's get a present for Eva."

"For you," he says. "For us."

We go into a store. Coats and coats. Sealskins, minks, ermine. I shrug them on and off, and I remember my mother, how I stroked her coats when I was a little girl, but I am here, not there, I am both places, everywhere, I slip skins on and off, but always, underneath, the core of self stands, and the coats lie heaped on the ground.

We leave. We leave with a tiny black purse, which I will never use but which Jacob says will be excellent for storing pot. Some gift. We laugh. We are a little drunk. A poor cat cries on the sidewalk.

Back at home, the baby is asleep. We pay forty dollars overtime and tiptoe in to see her. Then we make love on the mattress in the nursery, right beneath her crib. It is good, muscular sex, and I hold his hair in my two fists, and it is over.

After sex, sometimes, little stars swim. Sometimes, after sex, my cesarean scar hurts, and I don't know why this is so. I touch the thick scar. A cat cries and a rose grows. The baby mewls and Jacob brings her to me. He lays her on my naked stomach, as though she's just been born, the birth I wish I'd had, my body full of feeling, my legs strong and open, and we three lie, here at the very beginning, not a triangle or a line—there is curvature, a rounding out. A cat cries and a rose grows, and for now, for a very short time, maybe we are some kind of circle.

LETTER TO EVA
AT ONE YEAR

Dear Eva,

You were born on June 10, at 10:10 P.M., under the sign of Gemini. Astrologers say that night seven stars were aligned, and Jupiter was ringed with fire. Weathermen say storms were sweeping the Carolinas, and California blazed with heat, but here in Boston, your city of crooked streets and fruit markets, the wind was gentle, the tide just coming in. Right from the start your papa called you Caribou, because you had a touch of tundra in you, something otherworldly, but soft. The first story you heard was when you were only one hour old, wrapped in a striped cotton blanket. Your papa leaned into you and told you a tale called Grandfather Twilight, about a white-bearded gentleman who every evening tosses a pearl into the sky, whereupon it becomes the moon. If, when you are older, you look up at the night and feel a warm wash in your heart, it may be because this story lives in your memory.

As for me, Eva, know this. Although it took many, many months, twelve to be exact, I have at last come to feel a real passion for you, a passion slow growing and all the stronger for it. You are one year old today. You are 365 days on this earth, eighty-seven hundred and sixty hours. And late last night, driving back from a reading, having been away from you since dawn, I felt what I can only call a craving. I sped down the highway, because I had to get to you. Streetlights blurred by, birds called in the sky, but the world, then, was only you, and I realized that I had fallen, at long last, into the trough of love.

You, my child, are delightful. You have nothing wrong with you, and so many, many things right. The first object you ever reached for was an apple, Eva Claire, you are drawn to brightness and circles. You sometimes laugh in your sleep. You have the gift of gaze, a quiet, steady attention that lets you study the veining of a leaf, the weave of our rug with an intensity I admire. Seeing your timely progression through all the development milestones— turning over, sitting up, standing, first single steps— I sometimes find myself wondering now, one year out, if the Prozac I took was not a little like a vitamin. I spent nine months of pregnancy and so many months thereafter thinking of it as a toxin, but who's to say those little spheres did not in some way add folds to your brain, give greenness to your eyes.

Not that you won't have problems. We were at the pediatrician's the other day, for your one-year checkup, and the doctor said, given my own spotty mental health history, that we would have to watch you closely for any signs of disturbance. I nodded, but only out of politeness. Inside I was laughing at that doctor, because, over the course of coming to know you, I have also come to understand, in my maternal heart, that you are really okay. There are your eyes, moss green and woody, your delightful smile, the scrumptious pad of your cheek, which you like to lay against me. You are a girl so full of affection, it is a gift. Keep it with you as you move through time.

I want to be honest with you. When I think of my own mother, your grandmother Judith, I can come up with only blankness, a swirling white space at once silent and stormy. I want, Eva, for you to have me not as silence but as story. I have written, so far, three books, and you can find them in our living room, on the third shelf up. In the basement, behind the boiler, are twenty wire-bound journals, a lock of your great-grandmother's frost white hair, a family tree I have drawn, tracing your lineage back to the seamstress Mindle, and, in a still smaller, locked box, a paper on which I have written three secrets I wish to tell no one but you. When you are old enough, I will give you the key. It is, Eva, the key to me, and you may do with it as you wish.

I fear I will not always be there for you, and for this I apologize ahead of time. Early on in this story I asked if a mentally ill woman could be a good mother. I still don't know the answer. All I do know is that my life has been marked, and marred, by gaps of dysfunctions, times when I am, as they say, in hospital. In bed. Know this. You have a remarkably dedicated father. He will fill in. And I will always be there, even if I'm not there, even if I'm on some ward or in a crazy cloud, I won't forget you, Eva. I will come back to you. Always.

As for you, you have moss green eyes. And many gifts.

And while I chuckle at the pediatrician implying you are genetically loaded for illness, I also feel a little fear. I was speaking at a conference a few months ago, for parents of mentally ill children. "Do you worry about your own child?" the participants asked me. "I believe," I said, "that there are more and more treatment options coming down the pipeline. By the time my child is old enough to experience difficulties, I think her treatment choices will be very broad. I remain," I said, "cautiously optimistic."

About the future of treatments for serious mental illness, I am cautiously optimistic. About you, Eva, I am incautiously optimistic. You will go forward. You will make meaning. I hope my hair, my touch, the sound of my voice, and the smell of my skin are woven into whatever you do in the world. I hope what every parent hopes, to be carried by the child we carried, to be loved into infinity.

Today, Eva, it is your one-year birthday. Your first word was *door.* Your second word was *couscous.* Your third word was *Lila.* A child's first words must have some special significance. Door. An aperture, an opening. Or something that swings shut, seals you off. Couscous, well, the symbolism of that is beyond me. But Lila, the name of our dog, is the Hebrew word for night as well. Lila Lila Lila, you sing, as though you find the night beautiful, not scared by blackness, at home with the howl and the wolf.

You have learned, as well, to eat with a spoon, and to kiss, but you will not say bye-bye. Bye Bye Bye, I say, lifting your little arm, trying to teach you this trick of separation, this essential human milestone that marks the gateway to loneliness, to death. You will have none of it. You remain here, with us, your fists clenched closed, stubbornly in and of this world.

I hope many things for you, Eva. I hope, most of all, that you find real friends in this world. I hope you have a child of your own someday, and that, if you do, this book will be of some help, give you permission, perhaps—if you even need it—to experience the nine gestational months for what they are: intense, full of imaginings, full of fear, flutters, faces that pass before your eyes and then recede, slow-growing connections, wilting things, worry, worry, worry, a ring of fire, a wasteland of waiting, a self about to be new, becoming mother, the contours so slowly shaping themselves, you are lost. The baby is found. Infinity emerges. You learn about love, and the limits of your own flesh.

I am your mother, Eva. I am thirty-seven years old, not a young mother, not by any stretch. I will be very, very old, or even long gone, when you are in your thirties, or forties. For sure, your midlife will be without me. I will probably die in all sorts of small ways before that, though; I will die in spells of self-centeredness, of illness, of ambition, of the need for pure privacy and the pull of all my maternal ambivalence, of drowsy-making drugs. I want to tell you where to find me. Say *Lila Lila Lila* three times, say it deep in my ear, or, if I am not here, say it in a shell, and one way or another, I will make my way back to you, one way or another, I will hear.

I love you.

Happy first birthday, you with a touch of tundra, you of the red apple and dark night. We have made for you, today, a piñata, a pregnant piñata stuffed so full with bright candies. Later on today, we will hit the piñata with a stick, hit it high up in the tree, and at last it will happen, if we work hard enough, if we wait long enough, at last the casing will give way, the belly will break open, and from inside the animal, all this hard sweetness will pour.

Be well, my girl. *Be well.*

Love,
Your Mother

ABOUT THE AUTHOR

A 1999 National Magazine Award nominee, LAUREN SLATER has a master's degree in psychology from Harvard University and a doctorate from Boston University. Her work was chosen for *The Best American Essays/ Most Notable Essays* of 1994, 1996, 1997, 1998, and 1999. She is the winner of the 1993 New Letters Literary Award in creative nonfiction and of the 1994 Missouri Review Award. Her previous book, *Lying*, was chosen by *Entertainment Weekly* as one of the top ten best nonfiction books of 2000. Slater lives with her family in Massachusetts.

ABOUT THE TYPE

This book was set in Weiss, a typeface designed by a German artist, Emil Rudolf Weiss (1875–1942). The designs of the roman and italic were completed in 1928 and 1931 respectively. The Weiss types are rich, well-balanced, and even in color, and they reflect the subtle skill of a fine calligrapher.